Postiy

# Apostles Today

## *Christ's Love Gift to the Church*

### Barney Coombs

**Sovereign World**

Sovereign World Ltd
PO Box 777
Tonbridge
Kent TN11 9XT
England

ISBN: 1 85240 189 3

Typeset by CRB Associates, Norwich
Printed in England by Clays Ltd, St Ives plc

# Dedication

To the memory of W.F.P. Burton
– a spiritual father to many
and a twentieth-century apostle.

# Acknowledgements

It is never possible for any of us to adequately cover the list of all those who have influenced and helped to shape our lives and ministry. Some have done this through their preaching and others through their writings, but the most valuable contribution has come from those men and women whose friendship, loyalty and covenant love has helped to keep me close to the Lord and committed to the vision of seeing Jesus glorified in his church, and his kingdom come on earth in the power of the Holy Spirit.

Each time I stop and think about it, I always end up feeling overwhelmed by God's goodness to me. I am one blessed man – a beautiful and precious wife; two sons and a daughter whom any man would be proud of – and each of them married to wonderful partners. And to put the icing on the cake: seven delightful grandchildren who constantly light up my life.

Just writing this down is causing hallelujahs to rise up inside.

I am grateful to all those who have helped me to put this book together. To Bob Mumford, a close and dearly loved friend of twenty years standing, who has had a major impact on everything I preach and who has been gracious enough to spend precious time writing the foreword.

To my good friend Art Enns who has taken the entire manuscript and revamped it. To my dear and trusted friend Lucy Smith, who has painstakingly corrected the grammar. To Gina Charsley, my secretary and personal assistant for all her help in preparing the manuscript for editing and publication. To David Richards, Fraser Hardy and Ron MacLean who wrote testimonies on the benefits of having church reviews. To David and Rosemary Freeman, Bob and Muriel Whitchurch and Chris Richards who all helped in editing the rough copy. And finally, to my friend and pastor, Stephen Thomas, who has given me such helpful and scholarly counsel as this book has progressed towards its completion.

# Contents

# Foreword

This is a needed book. In fact, you will discover it to be somewhat more than the title suggests. I envisioned something of a polemic, an apologetic, perhaps a doctrinal treatise on the biblical necessity of apostolic authority. What we will discover is a heart-warming appeal from a spiritual father whose vision for a kind of New Testament Christianity will thrill your soul and call you up.

As you will see, Barney's working definition of an apostle is a 'problem solver'. He is one sent to attempt to 'solve the unsolvable' for the purpose of facilitating the increase of the Church of Jesus Christ in quality as well as quantity. It is Jesus Christ who 'builds his Church' and the apostle, particularly, has the overall responsibility to remove the obstacles which prevent this from occurring.

The author presents some practical and workable ideas as to the function of the apostolic office, as well as some rather innovative ideas as to the use of the apostolic anointing, such as, local apostles, fathering apostles, consultative leadership, and whether or not a person is a 'clinger' or a 'kisser'. Certainly, if you or I attempted to write this book, we would describe these things differently. My strong and over-riding impression, however, is that Barney's pastoral heart and passion for Christ and his Kingdom allows us to ignore whatever minor objections one may feel. My prayer is that any 'exceptions' we might note will not damage the joy of embracing the message and content of this book.

The author's cogent arguments, which are conciliatory in nature, seek to establish the irrefutable evidence that every biblical statement for the offices of pastor, and teacher and even evangelist for that matter, are inextricably linked to the offices of apostle and prophet. Their separation, the author says, can only be made an artificial and non-scriptural division between these needed offices.

Barney moves into areas of personal holiness, hidden motivations and relational maturity which are seen as increasingly critical for a healthy Church life. He asks some hard questions. Questions which, in my opinion, desperately need to be asked of all our Church leaders in the whole western world. Apostolic fathers, the author argues, is God's chosen route for us to see the reappearance and restoration of personal integrity. Unless this happens, we are in serious trouble.

Read carefully and with discernment what Barney has written. Consider biblically and presuppositionally that for which he is asking. This small book may give us the needed insight, perhaps the guidance and courage to adjust some of our deep-seated religious prejudices. It may, as well, allow us the needed freedom to recognise God's gifting which he has identified as apostles. Surely, the gentle and forthright manner in which this appeal is made, will honour our Lord Jesus Christ, further his Kingdom and modify some of our 'know-it-all' attitudes.

*Bob Mumford*
'Life Changers'
Raleigh, NC
USA

# Introduction

> *'It was he* (Christ) *who gave some to be apostles, some to be prophets, some to be evangelists, and some to be pastors and teachers, to prepare God's people for works of service, so that the body of Christ may be built up **until** we all reach unity in the faith and in the knowledge of the Son of God and become mature, attaining to the whole measure of the fulness of Christ.'*
> (Ephesians 4:11–13)

The premise of this book is that the church has not yet attained to *'the whole measure of the fulness of Christ'*; therefore the ministry gifts of Christ – apostles, prophets, evangelists, pastors and teachers – are still being given to the church, and are needed as much today as they were in the first century.

Some would argue that with the coming of the New Testament Scriptures, the need for apostles and prophets ceased, but there is no biblical evidence for such a view. Neither is there any historical evidence that the church has somehow outgrown the Ephesians 4 ministry gifts: that these gifts have become nonessential or superfluous. Rather, our danger is that we mistakenly consider ourselves rich and not in need of anything – much like a

11

modern day church of Laodicea.[1] But an honest look at the condition of the body of Christ today reveals both our powerlessness and our poverty. The truth is: we cannot afford to do without **any** of Christ's gifts, including – as I hope to demonstrate in the upcoming chapters – the work and ministry of apostles.

This book is not intended to be a comprehensive theological treatise on apostles (though such a text could be very helpful); neither is it written as an historical review of apostles through the ages. It is, very simply, a biblical outline of the role and function of apostles, together with a practical application for the church today.

I am aware, of course, that many evangelical leaders either dismiss the entire notion of modern day apostles or else ignore the issue in somewhat uncomfortable silence. We're used to leadership titles such as *President*, *Board Chairman*, *District Superintendent*, and *Conference Moderator* (or in other church circles *Archdeacon*, *Archbishop* and *Cardinal*). But calling someone an *Apostle*? Isn't that like claiming infallibility or something? Even some Bible translators equivocate over the use of this term, substituting the word *messenger* for *apostle*, presumably because it doesn't quite fit someone's theological predispositions.

The labels we apply to leaders and ministries may not be of ultimate importance (although I do question why we think *our* terminology is better than God's), but it *is* critical that we learn to do things God's way, especially when it comes to building in the church of Jesus Christ. If we do not recognise and receive one of the key ministry gifts of Christ to the church, we will (at best) build ineffectually.

This book is also intended to help 'de-mythologize' the role of apostle: to deal with the aura and mystique that some may associate with this ministry. While certain people tend to criticise and denigrate apostles (note Paul's need to defend his ministry to the Corinthians), others may almost deify them.

In this regard, I will always remember the words of a man who was a spiritual father to me, W.F.P. Burton. Willie Burton helped to plant nearly 1,500 churches in what was formerly known as the Belgian Congo, yet he always maintained a humble, down-to-earth view of himself and the 'great' apostles of Bible times. He offers this perspective – borne out of much godly wisdom and personal experience:

> 'When as a little boy I was taken to church, there was a coloured window in the end of the building showing the twelve apostles. They were dressed in most elaborately decorated robes, and carried croziers, orbs, lambs and other unnatural symbols in their hands, while round their heads were great halos, something like Lancashire cheeses. I sat looking at that window Sunday after Sunday, until I really thought that apostles were like that – but they were not. It was sheer imagination.
>
> Let me give you a Bible picture of an apostle: He is a weak little chap with a poor voice (2 Corinthians 10:10), a jailbird (Acts 16:23). He looks under-nourished and his clothing is disreputable (1 Corinthians 4:11). If you look at his hands, they are stained and cracked by the hard work of softening skins and sewing them into tents, for that is his livelihood (Acts 18:3). At times he is very ill, even despairing of life (2 Corinthians 1:8–11; Galatians 4:13; 2 Corinthians 11:30). Perhaps these infirmities have come from the terrible sufferings which he has undergone (2 Corinthians 11:23–28). That picture has not much in common with the twelve complacent

old gentlemen looking benignly at one from the church window, has it!'

The apostles whom Christ gives to the church are neither rogues nor super-saints. They are not relics of church history or figments of someone's imagination. They are men called of God to a particular ministry – a ministry that has been foundational to the church of the past and that will be essential to the church of the future. It has been my conviction for the past thirty years that without this ministry, the church cannot fulfil her destiny as God's instrument to bring the glory and the knowledge of the Lord to the whole earth.

I will endeavour to show from Scripture not only that apostles are intended for today, but also that they are indispensable in God's plan for the church. There is simply no substitute. This is still the 'Apostolic Age'.

### Footnote

[1]  Christ's words to that church were: *'You say, "I am rich; I have acquired wealth and do not need a thing." But you do not realise that you are wretched, pitiful, poor, blind and naked'* (Revelation 3:17).

# *Chapter 1*

## New Testament Apostles

There are twenty-two people named as apostles in the New Testament.[1] In contrast, there is only one pastor named: the Lord Jesus Christ, who is the 'Chief Shepherd (Pastor)'.[2] The term *pastor* is used only once as a noun in the New Testament,[3] and nowhere do we find references to a pastor leading a congregation. That is not to suggest that pastors did not carry an important function in first century church life, but rather to make the point that they appeared to occupy a less prominent role than they do today, serving alongside prophets, evangelists, teachers and apostles.

The word *apostle* as a noun comes from the Greek word *apostolos*, which literally means 'one sent forth'. It is first found in maritime language, referring to a cargo ship or fleet being sent out. Early usage of this term carried the twofold sense of *an express commission* and *being sent overseas.*

In his *Theological Dictionary of the New Testament*, Kittel[4] points out that *apostello*, the verb form, means *to send out* or *to send forth*, with emphasis on the sender – underscoring the idea of authorisation, as in the case of official envoys or divinely-sent teachers. Thus its use was not limited to the notion of travelling overseas. He points out that in the *Septuagint* there are more than 700 instances of *apostello*, and each time the word carried the idea of being sent with a commissioning, the emphasis being on the sender. An example of this is found in Isaiah 6:8 where the Lord is recorded as saying: *'Whom shall I send, and who will go for us?'* Isaiah then replies: *'Here am I. Send me!'* Kittel explains that in Greek Judaism, the term rarely occurs in reference to overseas travel since the Jews were not a seafaring people. Josephus uses it once for envoys sent to Rome which involved a journey by sea (*apostolos*).

In the sense of being sent in an official capacity, there is a link between *apostello* and the later institution of *salu(a)h*: a commissioning for a specific task with the emphasis on authorisation (the one sent representing the sender) – as in the case of Paul in his pre-Christian endeavours:

> *'Now Saul, still breathing threats and murder against the disciples of the Lord, went to the high priest, and asked for letters from him to the synagogues at Damascus, so that if he found any belonging to the Way, both men and women, he might bring them bound to Jerusalem.'* (Acts 9:1–2)

Kittel adds that the New Testament use of the word *apostle* always signified that the commissioned person was sent with full authority:

> 'It can refer to the commissioned representative of a congregation as in Philippians 2:23, where Paul writes, *"But I thought it necessary to send to you Epaphroditus, my brother and fellow-worker and fellow-soldier, who is also your messenger* (apostolos) *and minister to my needs."* Or it denotes the bearers

16

of the New Testament message: first the twelve (Acts 1:26), then the first Christian missionaries (Acts 14:4, 14), then to a wider circle (1 Corinthians 15:7).

The apostle is properly an apostle of Jesus Christ (rather than being sent by a local congregation), hence the emphasis on a meeting with the risen Lord to be personally commissioned. Apostles, then, are not officials of the church, but officers of Christ for its upbuilding, and in this sense they are comparable to the Old Testament prophets.'[5]

In summary, the word *apostle* in its earliest Greek form was a nautical term, referring to a freighter or naval force. Later, it came to include a person commissioned as an envoy. In the Synoptic Gospels, it was used of the 12 disciples personally commissioned by Jesus to be the vanguard of those sent to proclaim the good news – first to Jerusalem, then to all the nations of the world.[6] In addition, there were those who were assigned or seconded by the local church to serve a senior apostle, as in the case of Epaphroditus who served Paul on behalf of the church at Philippi.[7]

In the New Testament Epistles, apostles are mentioned in two other contexts: in Ephesians 4, where Paul outlines the *equipping gifts* and their place and function in the universal church; and in 1 Corinthians 12, where Paul refers to the various *ministries* (apostles, administrators, workers of miracles, interpreters of tongues, etc.), as necessary parts of the body of Christ in the context of its expression as the local church. These references provide the clearest link between apostles of biblical times and those of modern times, and will be the basis for further consideration in the following chapters.

We began this chapter by referring to the twenty-two (or more) apostles named in the New Testament. The list begins with the first and greatest apostle, Jesus Christ, who in turn chose the Twelve. To that initial group of *thirteen* apostles are added the following:

- *Matthias* – who replaced Judas as a member of the Twelve (Acts 1:24–26), but of whom very little is recorded.
- *Barnabas and Paul* – first called apostles by Dr Luke in Acts 14:4 and 14.
- *Epaphroditus* – clearly named in Philippians 2:25 – though some Bible translators choose the term *messenger* rather than the correct (literal) rendering *apostle*.
- *Silas and Timothy* – whose apostleship is established when Paul includes them in his salutation to the church in Thessalonika (1 Thessalonians 1:1), continues using the plural form *we* and *us*, then goes on to say in chapter 2 verse 6: '... *even though as apostles of Christ we might have asserted our authority.*'
- *James, the brother of Christ* – referred to by Paul in Galatians 1:19 as follows: '*But I did not see any other of the apostles except James, the Lord's brother.*' In chapter 2 verse 9 he includes this James along with Peter and John as pillars of the church.
- *Andronicus and Junias* – in Romans 16:7, Paul describes them as '*outstanding among the apostles.*'[8]

There are also several individuals whose apostleship could be inferred from the context of Scripture and/or their role in the early church. For example, Paul refers to *Titus* and a certain unnamed famous brother in 2 Corinthians 8:16–18 and 23:

'*But thanks be to God, who puts the same earnestness on your behalf in the heart of Titus. For he not only accepted our appeal, but being himself very earnest, he has gone to you of his own accord. And we have sent along with him the brother whose fame in the things of the gospel has spread through all the churches. As for Titus, he is my partner and fellow-worker among you; as for our brethren, they are messengers* (apostolos) *of the churches, a glory to Christ.'*

Some would add Apollos to the list in view of 1 Corinthians 4:6–13 where Paul, while speaking of himself and Apollos, says in verse 9: *'For, I think, God has exhibited us apostles last of all...'*

But there would seem to be many more apostles in the Bible than those we can identify easily by name. In the next chapter, we shall consider some of the *categories* of apostles we find in the pages of the New Testament.

## *Footnotes*

[1] These twenty-two (plus a few other names often added to the list) are noted at the end of this chapter.

[2] 1 Peter 5:4.

[3] Ephesians 4:11.

[4] R. Kittel, *Theological Dictionary of the New Testament*.

[5] *Ibid.*

[6] Matthew 28:18–20 and Acts 1:8.

[7] Philippians 2:25, 4:18.

[8] Chapter 10 addresses the issue of whether Junias was a man or a woman.

# *Chapter 2*

# Categories of Apostles

## *The* Apostle

The writer to the Hebrews admonishes us to *'consider Jesus, the Apostle and High Priest of our confession'*:[1] to *'fix your thoughts on Jesus, the apostle and high priest we confess.'*[2] *If we want to see an apostle par excellence,* we need go no further than Jesus himself. Sent by the Father, he travelled from the 'home base' of Heaven to the space-time world of Planet Earth. Anointed with the Holy Spirit, he was commissioned to preach the Gospel. He functioned in the full authority of his Father.

He not only laid a doctrinal foundation, he *was* the foundation. He was the ultimate builder: what he builds is indestructible and the gates of Hell and all the councils of Satan will not prevail against it. Signs and wonders accompanied his ministry. His apostleship was and is incomparable! Small wonder, then, that the definite article is used as he is proclaimed to be '*the* Apostle'.

## The three disciples

Peter, James[3] and John were part of the 'Twelve', but they clearly occupied a unique role among the disciples. Jesus distinguished between the 'Three' and the 'Twelve' on several important occasions: when he allowed Peter, James and John to view his transfiguration (and forbade them from telling others about it until the Resurrection); when he took only the Three with him when he raised the daughter of Jairus from the dead; and when he chose these Three to be with him in the Garden of Gethsemane in his moment of greatest agony.

Both Peter and John were used by the Holy Spirit to write important parts of Scripture. And James, conspicuous as a prominent, influential apostle, caught the attention of Herod Agrippa, who had him put to death by the sword – the first recorded Christian martyrdom.

## The Twelve Apostles of the Lamb

Besides Peter, James and John, the Twelve Apostles included: Andrew the brother of Peter; Philip; Bartholomew; Thomas; Matthew the tax-gatherer; James the son of Alphaeus; Thaddaeus; Simon the Zealot; and Judas Iscariot. With the exception of Judas, these eleven (plus one other) are those whose names are written on the twelve foundation stones of the New Jerusalem, and are known as the Twelve Apostles of the Lamb.[4]

That these men should be so honoured is an extraordinary demonstration of the grace of God: impatient and Christ-denying Peter, revengeful and ambitious James and John, unbelieving Thomas, dense and undiscerning Philip. What a motley crew! Paul says it perfectly in 1 Corinthians 1:27–28:

> 'But God has chosen the foolish things ... the weak things ... the base things ... the despised ... the things that are not, that he might nullify the things that are.'

Each stone in Revelation 21:19–20 is a precious jewel;

each one has become an object of beauty and priceless value. We can be assured that by the time he has finished *'working in us both to will and to do of his good pleasure,'*[5] we will be *'holy and blameless before him.'*[6] I love it! He takes beggars and turns them into princes. He gets hold of six foul-mouthed fishermen, a despised tax-gatherer and five other nobodies, and transforms them into the elite of Heavenly Jerusalem. That is miraculous, marvellous, magnificent grace!

Even apart from their elevation in the 'grand finale' as Apostles of the Lamb, these twelve are unique among the apostles referred to in Scripture and any other apostles in history. They were chosen by God to be witnesses of the life, death and resurrection of Christ. To them Jesus entrusted his teachings, which in turn had to be faithfully and accurately communicated – mostly by word of mouth – to the infant church. (Not that the Twelve were to accomplish this task on their own: Jesus promised to send the Holy Spirit to live in them and empower them.) They were the first missionaries: the vanguard of those sent to proclaim the Gospel of the Kingdom to the ends of the earth. Last, but not least, they are the first-born on Planet Earth of the new creation in Christ.

## The seventy

In Luke chapter 9 we find the account of Jesus sending out the twelve apostles, giving them power and authority to proclaim the kingdom of God, to cast out demons and to heal diseases. One chapter later we read of him sending out another group:

> *Now after this the Lord appointed seventy*[7] *others and sent them two by two ahead of him to every city and place where he himself was going to come.'*

Jesus then gives them instructions and a mandate:

> *'And whatever city you enter, and they receive you, eat what is set before you; and heal those in it who are sick, and say to them, "The kingdom of God has come near to you." Behold I have given you authority to tread upon serpents and scorpions, and over all the power of the enemy, and nothing shall injure you.'*
>
> (Luke 10:8–9, 19)

Considering the similarities between this account and the sending of the twelve, the characteristic meanings of the verb *apostello* and the noun *apostolos*, and the criteria for apostles previously laid out, it would not seem to be stretching a point too far if we called the seventy *apostles*. In referring to the resurrected Christ and those who saw him, Paul says:

> *'After that he appeared to more than five hundred brethren at one time, most of whom remain until now, but some have fallen asleep; then he appeared to James, then to all the apostles . . .*
>
> (1 Corinthians 15:6–7)

Is Paul referring to the seventy when he says 'all the apostles'? That is what some commentators would suggest. The *Commentary on the Whole Bible* by Jamieson, Fausset and Brown notes:

> 'The term here includes many others besides "the Twelve" already enumerated (v. 5): perhaps the seventy disciples (Luke 10).'[8]

In his interpretation of the phrase 'all the apostles', Adam Clarke comments,

'...including not only the eleven, but as some
suppose, the seventy-two disciples.' [9]

## Equipping Apostles

Ephesians chapter 4 speaks of ministries as gifts:

> *'When he ascended on high, he led captives in his train
> and gave gifts to men. It was he who gave some to be
> apostles, some to be prophets, some to be evangelists,
> and some to be pastors and teachers.'*

> (Ephesians 4:8, 11)

While the terms *Fivefold Ministries or Ascension Gifts*
are used for those listed in verse 11, I prefer to call them
*Equipping Ministries* because they were given to equip the
saints for works of service. [10]

If we see *equipping* in terms of others being prepared or
trained to do the work, it follows that the Ephesians 4
apostle is one who equips the church to function
apostolically. More specifically, he would be expected to
teach, correct and advise apostles-in-training (i.e. *junior*
apostles). If this is true, we should see evidence of this
training process in the New Testament.

In fact, there are many examples of this type of apostle,
beginning with the twelve while they were being discipled
by Jesus. His first words to them contain a ministry goal –
*'Follow me and I will make you fishers of men'* (Mark 1:17),
while his final instructions carry a mandate to continue
the work – *'As the Father has sent me, I also send you'*
(John 20:21).

Then we have Paul's letters to Timothy and Titus –
which are commonly known as the 'Pastoral Epistles'
even though they are clearly apostolic in nature. It was no
doubt in consequence of Paul's grave concerns about

'savage wolves' coming to steal some of the Ephesian flock [11] that he decides to leave Timothy at Ephesus *'in order that you may instruct certain men not to teach strange doctrine'* (1 Timothy 1:3), as well as to provide clear instructions on other foundational issues such as the character qualifications for elders, deacons and deaconesses.[12] Timothy thus became an extension of Paul's apostolic ministry to that church.

To Titus he writes:

> *'For this reason I left you in Crete, that you might set in order what remains, and appoint elders in every city as I directed you.'* (Titus 1:5)

Then, as with Timothy, Paul goes on to list the necessary qualifications for elders, as well as focusing on other apostolic issues such as the upholding of sound doctrine. In these three letters we find a senior apostle addressing his spiritual sons whom he has left behind in Ephesus and Crete with the mandate of carrying out apostolic business: in other words, a chief apostle instructing and equipping junior apostles.

## Local Apostles

In 1 Corinthians 12:28 we find a list of ministries which starts with apostles and ends with those speaking in various kinds of tongues.[13] The context of this passage is Paul addressing the behaviour of the Corinthian church members when they come together. It seems clear from these chapters – 1 Corinthians 11 to 14 – that Paul is dealing with issues pertaining to the local church. The speakers in tongues were not trans-local (at least there is no suggestion here or anywhere else that this ministry was trans-local); neither, would I submit, were these apostles trans-local.

By most estimates, the church at Corinth numbered in the thousands [14] when this was written. In the same way that certain apostles lived and carried out their senior leadership responsibilities in Jerusalem, [15] it is not too difficult to assume that a city church of that size would also have resident apostles. In the case of Ephesus, we know that Paul remained there for three years and that Timothy's tenure was probably the same. Since they did not cease to be apostles during their extended stay, they evidently functioned as local apostles for that period of time.

## Ethnic Apostles

Galatians 2:7–9 relates an interesting development in apostolic strategy in the early church. Three apostles – James, Peter and John – were to have special responsibility in bringing the gospel to the Jews, while Paul and Barnabas were recognised as apostles to the Gentiles.

Could this approach be effective in our multicultural cities of the 20th century? I believe it could. I see no reason why God could not use the same strategy these days: to prepare and 'set apart' an apostle to take the gospel to a particular ethnic group (especially if this was also a distinct language group). There have been a number of prophecies in recent years saying that the Lord would be sending missionaries to the West. Who knows? In God's economy, we may yet see an apostle from India invited to work among the Asian community in places like Bradford or Walsall.

## Fathering Apostles

According to Paul's writings in 1 Corinthians 4:14–17 and Titus 1:4, he was a spiritual father to the church at

Corinth and a spiritual father to Timothy and Titus. A father is one who not only teaches you, but also provides a role model; thus Paul could say to his Corinthian children:

> *'For in Christ Jesus I became your father through the gospel. I exhort you therefore, be imitators of me.'*[16]

That exhortation could easily be misunderstood as a clumsy attempt at control, but Paul qualifies it in the next verse by pointing out that the things he wants them to imitate are his ways in Christ. The church today has a great need of fathering apostles. We will consider further this need in later chapters, and deal with some of the related practical issues.

## Serving Apostles

In recognising various kinds of biblical apostles, we must understand that these are *descriptive* categories rather than rigid classifications. For example, Timothy and Titus, whatever their other apostolic roles, could both be considered *serving* apostles. Paul says of Timothy, *'But you know of his proven worth that he served with me in the furtherance of the gospel like a child serving his father,'*[17] and of Titus, *'my true child in a common faith,'*[18] and *'my partner and fellow worker.'*[19] Epaphroditus is described by Paul as *'your apostle and minister to my need.'*[20]

It is generally agreed that Paul usually travelled with a sizeable team (which some would call an apostolic team). While Paul refers to them as fellow-workers, fellow-soldiers and even fellow-prisoners, it is clear from Scripture that they not only served *with* Paul, but also served *him*. Their roles were subordinate. Thus we find him saying to Timothy,

*'Pick up Mark and bring him with you, for he is useful to me for service. Tychicus I have sent to Ephesus. When you come, bring the cloak which I left at Troas with Carpus and the books, especially the parchments.'*[21]

Here and elsewhere in his letters, Paul is giving instructions as one who expects his directives to be obeyed.

It is important that we don't fall into the trap of viewing apostles as superstars. Paul, to be sure, was outstanding in his leadership and ministry, but if we think that all apostles must measure up to this exceptional standard, we are going beyond the evidence warranted by Scripture. There are not only different kinds of apostles, but also varying measures of faith and grace that accompany each ministry gift.[22] In the next chapter, however, we shall try to learn some key lessons in apostolic ministry from the portfolio of the man who called himself the *least* of the apostles – but from whom we have so much to learn – the apostle Paul.

### Footnotes

[1] Hebrews 3:1 *New American Standard Bible*.

[2] Hebrews 3:1 *New International Version*.

[3] This James and his brother John were the sons of Zebedee (as distinct from James the brother of the Lord).

[4] Revelation 21:14, Matthew 19:28. Matthias was chosen to replace Judas Iscariot, but whether he occupies that role in the New Jerusalem is not stated.

[5] Philippians 2:13.

[6] Ephesians 1:4.

[7] Luke 10:1 Some manuscripts read *seventy-two*.

[8] Jamieson, Fausset, Brown, *Commentary on the Whole Bible*.

[9] Adam Clarke, *Commentary*. See also footnote 7 re: *seventy-two*.

[10] Ephesians 4:12.

[11] Acts 20:29–31.

[12] 1 Timothy 3:1–13.

[13] While chapter 14 suggests that *all* can prophesy and speak in tongues, 1 Corinthians 12:28 refers to specific, recognised ministries. Thus speaking in tongues can be a personal devotional gift or it can be a *ministry* gift for the edification of the church.

[14] It may have numbered in the tens of thousands, given Corinth's estimated population of half a million.

[15] Acts chapter 15.

[16] 1 Corinthians 4:15–16.

[17] Philippians 2:22.

[18] Titus 1:4.

[19] 2 Corinthians 8:23.

[20] Philippians 2:25.

[21] 2 Timothy 4:11–13.

[22] Romans 12:3 and Ephesians 4:7.

# Chapter 3

## Paul, the Wise Master Builder

A lot of my discoveries of truth follow a certain pattern: I fail to notice something until it seems to jump out and hit me. Then once I see it, I cannot stop observing it: everywhere I turn, the evidence of my discovery is staring me in the face. Does this sound familiar?

That was how I 'discovered' 1 Corinthians 3:11 some years ago:

> *'For no man can lay a foundation other than the one which is laid, which is Jesus Christ.'*

In this verse, Paul is not only referring to Christ's incarnation, atoning death and resurrection; he also is saying that only in Christ can *anything* have eternal value. Verses 12–15 tell us that in Christ our 'building materials' are gold, silver and precious stones; outside of Christ they are wood, hay and stubble – destined to burn.

In the second half of 1 Corinthians 8:6 Paul declares that there is *'one Lord, Jesus Christ, through whom are all things, and we exist through him.'* As far as the apostle is concerned, everything that pertains to life must first of all be grounded in Christ, founded on Christ, resourced through Christ, motivated by Christ and exist for the glory of Christ.

Paul is so intent on bringing Christ into every observation and instruction – 'in the Lord', 'in Christ' and so on – that he almost sounds super-spiritual at times. But those phrases were not just repetitious words, they truly described the focus of his life. Galatians 2:20 sums it up beautifully:

> *'I have been crucified with Christ; and it is no longer I who live, but Christ lives in me; and the life which I now live in the flesh I live by faith in the Son of God, who loved me, and delivered himself up for me.'*

The heart of a true apostle will always be directed towards seeing Christ established at the centre. His overriding ministry goal will be that he might contribute – whether in a small way or a great way – to establishing *'an administration . . . that is the summing up of all things in Christ, things in the heavens and things upon the earth.'* [1]

We have a right to be suspicious of anyone who claims to be an apostle but who turns out to be more concerned with promoting his own ministry than promoting the Lord Jesus.[2] Paul could claim with full integrity: *'For I determined to know nothing among you except Jesus Christ, and him crucified,'* and again, *'For me to live is Christ.'* [3] What a magnificent confession!

## He built theologically

To the apostle Paul, building on Christ also meant building on the Word of God. In his farewell message to the Ephesian elders he says:

> *'For I did not shrink from declaring to you the whole purpose of God . . . And now I commend you to God*

31

and to the word of his grace, which is able to build you
up.'                                              (Acts 20:27, 32)

He likewise admonishes other apostles to use the Word of
God in their ministry, as we see in these excerpts from his
letters to Timothy:

> *'In pointing out these things to the brethren, you will be
> a good servant of Christ Jesus, constantly nourished on
> the words of the faith and of sound doctrine which you
> have been following. Until I come, give attention to the
> public reading of Scripture, to exhortation and teach-
> ing. Be diligent to present yourself approved to God as
> a workman who does not need to be ashamed, handling
> accurately the word of truth.'*
>
> (1 Timothy 4:6, 13 and 2 Timothy 2:15)

As Paul delivers what is, in effect, his last will and testament to his beloved Timothy, he underscores the critical
importance of building theologically:

> *'I solemnly charge you in the presence of God and of
> Jesus Christ, who is to judge the living and the dead,
> and by his appearing and his kingdom: preach the
> word; be ready in season and out of season; reprove,
> rebuke, exhort, with great patience and instruction.
> For the time will come when they will not endure sound
> doctrine; but wanting to have their ears tickled, they
> will accumulate for themselves teachers in accordance
> with their own desires.'*          (2 Timothy 4:1–3)

With the level of biblical illiteracy we see amongst
evangelicals today – particularly in some of the new
churches – such an exhortation is certainly relevant to our

generation. By and large, there is very little expository teaching taking place on a typical Sunday in our churches.

Also symptomatic of this problem, our Christian bookshops are carrying fewer books on theology and increasing numbers on psychology and counselling. Whatever happened to the biblical truth that we are new creatures in Christ? The first thing that happened to Adam and Eve after they fell was that they became *self*-conscious, *self*-absorbed. But as Christians we should be 'fixing our eyes upon Jesus'[4] – not turning from 'Son-gazing' to navel-gazing. The further we stray from the foundation of Jesus Christ, his redemptive work at Calvary and his word (the teachings of Scripture) the more susceptible we are to deception and introspection.

I recently heard reports about a 'Christian' counselling service that has developed a new therapy for people with multiple personality disorders: they address each personality as a distinct person and lead each one to repentance from sin and faith in Jesus. Think about it: five personalities, five conversions. I didn't ask if this was followed by five baptisms – or perhaps five consecutive communion services. What absolute rubbish! What unbiblical nonsense!

Once we abandon our scriptural foundations and no longer build theologically, we are left with subjectivity and relativism.[5] And that is precisely what I find invading not only our evangelical churches, but also our Christian magazines. I recently read an article in which a well-known, respected woman testified that she had now shifted her position on Paul's instruction that wives should be subject to their own husbands as to the Lord.[6] She now believes that marriage is to be a partnership and therefore the old position is no longer relevant.

Now, I have no problem with the idea of marriage as partnership, but I do find it deeply disturbing that a

Christian leader can simply dismiss a clear directive from Scripture just because it doesn't fit the current cultural pattern or her own changing opinions. If she had wrestled with the text and had concluded that it didn't actually mean what she had previously thought, I could at least respect her convictions. But to disregard a passage of Scripture as if it did not exist is cause for great concern.

Amongst the hindrances to building theologically are four that I heard described by Steve Harbridge, senior leader of Orillia Christian Fellowship in the province of Ontario in Canada. He posed the question 'How do we arrive at any one position of truth or conviction?' and then outlined four *wrong* ways:

## 1. The deception of our own perception

We may wrongly interpret Scriptures because of misperceptions and misunderstandings. Steve told of a young lad who asked his father for a dollar coin (called a *loonie* in Canada) in order to buy a can of cola from the vending machine. His father was perfectly happy to pay for the drink but he had only *quarters* (25 cent coins). The boy said, 'But Dad, there is a notice on the machine that says it only takes loonies.' After quite a strong discussion, the father took his son over to the machine and asked the lad to read the notice. It said: *'This machine will take loonies.'* The young fellow had mistakenly read *'only'* into the text.

Our perception of truth may also be distorted by our own preferences and predispositions. Some friends of mine claim that Romans 14:17 – *'for the kingdom of God is not eating or drinking, but righteousness and peace and joy in the Holy Spirit'* – means that we are free to eat and drink what we like, so long as we do it in faith. But a closer look at the context of that verse will show us that the point being made is a very different one, namely: the kingdom of God is so important, we dare not allow our freedom (in eating and drinking) to be a hindrance to others. The predisposition to reject anything which smacks of religious, legalistic rules is valid, but, mixed with the strength of our own preference to do as we please, it can lead us to 'read into' Scriptures meanings that are unsupported by the context.

## 2. *Influence by a well-known and highly respected person or by the pressure of the majority*

When our children started attending school, it wasn't long before we found ourselves being confronted with statements such as, 'Well, Miss Brown says it's all right' – meaning: if the teacher says it, it must be right! As adults we smile at such blind faith: we know that position and authority are no guarantee of truth. But in reality we are all tempted to be less critical of what we are taught by famous or well-respected people.[7] The same applies to majority opinion. When Janette and I are travelling a long distance by car we often look for an inn or hotel in the countryside for a meal. One of the telltale signs that an eating establishment provides good meals is the number of vehicles parked outside. Our reasoning is this: 'They can't all be wrong.' But do you know what? Sometimes they can.

## 3. *Negative experiences which determine our predispositions*

There are many people who reject the evangelical foundations (fundamentals) of the Christian faith because of the manner in which 'fundamentalists' argue their cause in the media. Such predispositions can affect one's eternal destiny. But there are others which affect how Christians relate to one another in the body of Christ. For example, I believe in *discipleship*. It's a good biblical term and an important biblical doctrine. But in some parts of North America and elsewhere, Christians would react negatively if they heard me use this word. I'm *reformed* in my theology, but again, that creates difficulty in some people's minds because of the arrogant manner in which some Calvinists hold forth their doctrine.

### 4. Reliance on tradition

Historically, reliance on tradition has proven to be a major hindrance in the search for truth and building *theologically*. Someone once said, 'Know what you believe, but know *why* you believe it.' History shows that people who obtain truth by revelation and understanding – people who *see* it – are usually willing, if necessary, to die for the truth. In contrast to these martyrs of the faith, people who receive truth only by tradition either end up losing it or trying to preserve it by carnal means such as persecuting (or even killing) others in order to protect their tradition.

## He built evangelistically

Paul's great passion was to preach the Gospel. He knew from the fourth day after his conversion that he was *'set apart for the gospel of God'* as he points out in Acts 9:15 and Romans 1:1. Within days of his dramatic encounter with Jesus we find him preaching Christ in the Damascus synagogues, boldly (even recklessly, given the circumstances) declaring Jesus to be the Son of God.

Paul seemed to jump at every opportunity to preach the good news. He writes to the believers in Rome and informs them that he is eager to preach the gospel in their city (Romans 1:15). He makes it clear that when he does visit them, it will not be in secret: *'I am not ashamed of the gospel,'* he challenges the Romans, *'for it is the power of God for salvation.'*[8] There was a deep, compelling motivation in Paul never to stop preaching – as we see in 1 Corinthians 9:16 where he exclaims, *'Woe is me if I do not preach the gospel.'*

Paul was what some would call a gospel lunatic! He would do almost anything to reach people with the gospel, as we see in this excerpt from his letter to the Corinthians:

> *'Though I am free and belong to no man, I make myself a slave to everyone, to win as many as possible. To the Jews I became like a Jew, to win the Jews. To those under the law I became like one under the law (though I myself am not under the law), so as to win those under the law. To those not having the law I became like one not having the law (though I am not free from God's law but am under Christ's law), so as to win those not having the law. To the weak I became weak, to win the weak. I have become all things to all men so that by all possible means I might save some. I do all this for the sake of the gospel, that I might share in its blessings.'*    (1 Corinthians 9:19–23)

I cannot help but smile as I write this section because it reminds me of my own father who is now with the Lord. In the last photograph taken of my father, he is seated in an armchair next to my mother, wearing his favourite red tie with the name *JESUS* proudly displayed down the front. He lived to age eighty-six, still active in his ministry. The night before he passed away, my father was out on the streets with my brother-in-law Ron, preaching the gospel. As fellow 'gospel lunatics', he and the apostle Paul are undoubtedly getting along just fine!

# He built patriarchally

Paul was a spiritual father who took his responsibilities very seriously, even if it meant defending his paternal role in the face of opposition. To the unruly Corinthians he writes:

> *'I am not writing this to shame you, but to warn you, as my dear children. Even though you have ten thousand guardians [9] in Christ, you do not have many fathers, for in Christ Jesus I became your father through the gospel. Therefore I urge you to imitate me.'*
>
> (1 Corinthians 4:14–16)

The concept of spiritual fatherhood is all but lost in the church today. Although Roman Catholics and Anglo-Catholics still use the term *father* when addressing their priests, such practice often bears little relationship to biblical fatherhood. As Paul points out in his admonition to the Corinthian church, there is a difference between those whose function is to give instruction as *guardians* or *tutors*, and those whose role it is to be spiritual *fathers*. A teacher's accountability toward God in terms of ministry centres around his handling of Scripture, whereas a spiritual father is accountable to God primarily for the *people* entrusted to his fathering care – a care that includes imparting to them his ways in Christ. (Paul, as we saw in the Scripture noted above, even urged his spiritual children to *imitate* him.)

As we examine Paul's letters, we soon discover other evidences of fatherhood: how a father reacts when his children are threatened, or how he feels when his most precious hopes and dreams for his children are being destroyed. Listen to these words written to the Galatian church:

> *'I am amazed that you are so quickly deserting him who called you by the grace of Christ for a different gospel ... If any man is preaching to you a gospel contrary to that which you received, let him be accursed.'*　　　　　　　　(Galatians 1:6, 9)

Later in Paul's letter, the tone changes from concern to alarm:

> *'You foolish Galatians, who has bewitched you? and My children, with whom I am again in labour until Christ is formed in you ... '*　　　(Galatians 3:1, 4:19)

Finally, so incensed with the false teachers who have intruded into his territory and caused such a disturbance among 'his children', Paul throws caution to the wind and clearly expresses his anger:

> *'Why don't these agitators, obsessive as they are about circumcision, go all the way and castrate themselves!'*
> (Galatians 5:12) [10]

Ouch! Imagine a pastor standing up on a Sunday morning and speaking like that to his congregation!

But as extreme as Paul's reaction may sound, as a father I can identify with those feelings. I remember when our daughter Rachel had just started attending the infant school just fifty yards from our home. She was only five years old, but had been attending long enough to feel confident about returning home unaccompanied after school ended. However one day she failed to turn up. Thirty minutes went by before I realised she was missing, so I rushed over to the school, arriving just in time to catch the caretaker locking the front door and preparing to leave. There was no sign of Rachel anywhere. At first I began to panic, but then the thought struck me: perhaps she went home with one of her school friends.

'Would you mind opening up the school office so I can check for the names and addresses of my little girl's friends?' I asked anxiously. 'Maybe she's gone home with one of them.'

'No, I haven't got time to do that,' the caretaker replied. 'I've finished for the day.'

At this point I'm afraid I lost my temper. 'Finished?' I shouted. 'Finished? I haven't even started!'

The caretaker's face turned a little pale as I put the issue to him in unmistakable terms: 'Now listen here, buddy. You have a choice: you can either open up the office voluntarily, or I will use whatever force is necessary to take the keys from you and do it myself.'

He quickly complied and opened up. As I had suspected, Rachel was indeed with one of her friends and everything turned out fine. But why had I reacted that way? The answer is simple: Rachel was my dearly-loved and greatly-valued child, I was her father, and she was possibly in danger. Even though I was a well-respected pastor in the town with a reputation to uphold, I was willing to do anything at that moment to ensure her safety. Had I been arrested for threatening to assault the caretaker and the incident reported in the newspaper, I think I would have cut out the news report, framed it, and hung it up for all to see. That's fatherhood – at least the Galatians chapter 5 kind!

For another dimension of fatherhood, observe how tenderly and intimately Paul writes to Timothy:

> *'To Timothy, my beloved son ... I constantly remember you in my prayers night and day, longing to see you, even as I recall your tears, so that I may be filled with joy.'* (2 Timothy 1:2–4)

We have no way of knowing Timothy's emotional state prior to receiving this letter, but we can safely assume that there were tears in his eyes after reading the opening lines. I have actually wept just thinking about how Timothy must have responded internally when he first read those words. Certainly he and Titus and Philemon must have treasured those personal letters they received from their spiritual father – as evidenced by the preservation and subsequent inclusion of Paul's letters as part of the New Testament.

## He built relationally

Paul was essentially a relational man. As F.F. Bruce describes it:

> (Paul) attracted friends around him as a magnet attracts iron filings. His genius for friendship has been spoken of so often that it has become proverbial – almost a cliché, in fact. There are about seventy people mentioned by name in the New Testament of whom we should never have heard were it not for their association with Paul, and over and above these, there is a host of unnamed friends.' [11]

Paul had a clear revelation that the Church, as the body of Christ, is essentially relational:

> *'For just as we have many members in one body and all do not have the same function, so we, who are many, are one body in Christ, and individually members of one another.'* (Romans 12:4–5)

It is in this context that he goes on to exhort the Roman Christians:

*'Let love be without hypocrisy ... Be devoted to one another in brotherly love ... Rejoice with those who rejoice and weep with those who weep. Be of the same mind toward one another; do not be haughty in mind, but associate with the lowly.'*

(Romans 12:9, 10, 15, 16)

To the Corinthians Paul says:

*'For even as the body is one and yet has many members, and all the members of the body, though they are many, are one body, so also is Christ.'*

(1 Corinthians 12:12)

Notice, he doesn't say 'like Christ', he says 'is Christ'. He does not separate the body from Christ but sees the body and the head as indivisible. This is spelled out even more clearly in Paul's letter to the Ephesians:

*'[S]peaking the truth in love, we are to grow up in all aspects into him, who is the head, even Christ, from whom the whole body, being fitted and held together by that which every joint supplies, according to the proper working of each individual part, causes the growth of the body for the building up of itself in love.'*

(Ephesians 4:14–16)

It is interesting to note that Paul includes relational matters in each of his epistles. Seen from the relational perspective, the list of twenty-seven names in Romans 16 is not an incidental add-on or *appendix* to his letter, but a heart-warming expression of his love and concern for people. For Paul, the church was not a physical structure or a gathering to be attended, but a *people* – God's redeemed people – who were being fitted together and growing together into a holy temple in the Lord Jesus.[12]

So much of today's gathered church activity is *event* oriented. As leaders, we might want to ask ourselves, 'Am I running an organisation, or am I building family? Do I see my responsibilities as being a professional job from which I can resign if things are not to my liking, or do I see that I am inseparably joined to these people "till death do us part"? Am I like Orpah who kissed her mother-in-law and left her, or like Ruth who clung to Naomi in covenant commitment? Am I in the pastor-swapping business or do I see myself as a permanent fixture?'

Charles, an Anglican curate and a dear friend of mine, was invited by his bishop to explain why he had not applied for a living[13] at another parish. Charles replied that God had joined him to the vicar of the parish in which he presently served, and that he was very happy and fulfilled in his ministry. The bishop enquired what he meant by the word *joined*; he had never heard of such a thing. The curate replied that his relationship to the vicar was similar to that of Timothy in relation to Paul: he was like a son serving his father in the gospel.

At a later date, the bishop sent for my friend a second time and reminded him that he had a responsibility to provide properly for his wife and six children – especially for his children's education. However, the bishop's concerns seemingly went unattended. But the job status of my friend did change eventually. He has since replaced the former vicar and is now himself in charge of the parish, doing a great job – just like his spiritual father had done before him.

A pastor once came to me and suggested that he come and work alongside me in order to be discipled. I pointed out that he had a flock to love and care for (it was, in fact, a church that he had started). 'Oh, that's nothing,' he said. 'I've started churches before and left them; it won't be too difficult to leave another one.' That was all I needed to hear. If you guessed that he didn't link up with me, you guessed correctly.

Is it any wonder that so many Christians are church-hoppers when so many pastors are church swappers? Of course, I'm not saying that God couldn't relocate a pastor. The problem is that so many leaders see pastoral transfers as a way of life, and for most denominations, it is their *modus operandi*. This problem is compounded by some of the advice given to aspiring pastors at Bible College or seminary: 'Now don't get too close to the members of your congregation; otherwise you will allow yourself to become vulnerable and lose the mystique of your leadership. Nor should your wife have any close friends in the congregation.'

Such thinking is clearly unbiblical and opposed to the relational leadership demonstrated by Paul. Here are some pertinent questions that a relational apostle might ask a pastoral leader to consider: 'What do I do that places me above – or apart from – those whom God has entrusted to my care? What do I say that places me above – or apart from – those whom God has entrusted to my care, and how do I say it? What do I wear, or what title do I allow myself to be called, that places me above – or apart from – those whom God has entrusted to my care?' The answers to these questions could well determine whether I'm building a family or just a religious corporation.

## He built supernaturally

Signs and wonders were a 'supernaturally natural' part of Paul's ministry. There is no record of controversy surrounding the practice of laying hands on the sick, nor had the term *the end of the apostolic age* been invented. The churches Paul founded were born into the realm of the supernatural and continued to experience supernatural phenomena. In his doctrinal argument with the Galatian church regarding faith, Paul alludes to miracles as normative:

> *'Does he then, who provides you with the Spirit and works miracles among you, do it by the works of the Law, or by hearing with faith?'* [14]

And he reminds the Corinthians that his ministry was accompanied by signs, wonders and miracles. [15]

It seems that for Paul, 'fully preaching the gospel' included a demonstration of God's power through signs and wonders:

> *'For I will not presume to speak of anything except what Christ has accomplished through me, resulting in the obedience of the Gentiles by word and deed, in the power of signs and wonders, in the power of the Spirit; so that from Jerusalem and round about as far as Illyricum I have fully preached the gospel of Christ.'*
>
> (Romans 15:18–19)

It was the sort of gospel that was preached by W.F.P. Burton, a 20th century apostle to the Belgian Congo. [16] In 1915 when he arrived at Mwanza in the heart of the Congo, Willie Burton was met by the chief and all the villagers, who were eager to see the strange white men who had suddenly appeared from down-river. Willie knew nothing of the native language, but he noticed that the old chief was nearly bent over double – obviously troubled with severe arthritis. As Willie described it to me years later:

'I stretched out my hand and placed it on the head of the old chap and said, "Father, in the name of Jesus, be pleased to heal this man," and instantly the old man straightened up. The rest of the villagers were utterly astonished and began to make a noise that sounded as if they had the hiccups.'

Needless to say, the white men were warmly welcomed to that village! On another occasion their welcome was a little too 'warm'. Willie and his wife had crossed over the river to take the gospel to a village notorious for cannibalism. Within moments of their arrival they were seized and bound to a tree to await their fate. Soon a fire was lit and a big pot placed on top of it. The natives started gathering around the Burtons and feeling their arms and legs, all the while licking their lips in eager anticipation of the sumptuous feast the Burtons were about to provide. Here is how Willie later described the scene:

'At this point, Sister Burton and I began to pray. I said, "Father, if this is the time for us to be taken home, then we are ready; but if it's not, then you will have to do something." Before I could hardly get the words out of my mouth, the chief collapsed on the ground, writhing in pain. Soon the witch-doctors were working all their magic charms, but to no effect. I began to call out, "Look, he's getting worse: he's going to die."'
"Shut up and be quiet!" they cried.
But I wasn't going to be quiet. So I called out, "If you were to ask me, I would pray to my God and he would heal your chief." They kept on trying their magic charms, but the chief was getting steadily worse. Eventually they came and requested my help.
"Not with us tied to this tree," I insisted.

Reluctantly they released us. I went over to the chief and prayed a simple prayer, asking Father to heal him in the name of Jesus. Immediately the chief recovered. As a result of this miracle I was able to preach the gospel to the whole village. Oh, what a privilege! At the end of my message, the chief was the first to confess Jesus as his Saviour. This was quickly followed by all his wives receiving the Lord Jesus. You know, it wasn't long before the entire village came to Christ and were baptised.'

As we see in the lives of apostles throughout the centuries, building supernaturally goes hand-in-hand with building evangelistically: signs and wonders are given in order to open hearts to the gospel and to validate the authority of Christ.

## He built pastorally

Although some believe that Paul's main 'ministry flow' was as a prophet or a teacher,[17] he faithfully demonstrated the caring heart of a pastor. A good pastor will always have a heart concern for the health and welfare of those allotted to his charge, diligently applying the principle of Proverbs 27:23:

> *'Know well the condition of your flocks and pay attention to your herds.'*

We find much evidence of this kind of concern in Paul's life and ministry. In the conclusion of his list of hardships and sufferings in 2 Corinthians 11:28–29, he adds this:

> *'Apart from such external things, there is the daily pressure upon me of concern for all the churches.'*

Note the words *daily* and *all*. It takes a shepherd's heart to care that way.

He continues:

> *'Who is weak without me being weak? Who is led into sin without my intense concern?'*

Note the word *intense*. This intensity was seldom more evident than when he wrote to Philemon on behalf of Onesimus:

> *'I have sent him back to you in person, that is, sending my very heart.'* [18]

As part of his care for the churches he planted, Paul ensured that elders were appointed in each of them [19] so that the flock of God would be adequately led and cared for. And to the elders he gives this charge:

> *'Be on your guard for yourselves and for all the flock, among which the Holy Spirit has made you overseers, to shepherd the church of God which he purchased with his own blood.'*                    (Acts 20:28)

Paul addresses a number of pastoral concerns in his letters to church leaders – 1 Timothy chapter 5 being a prime example. In verses one and two, Paul advises Timothy on how to address the older men and women in the church community properly, then on how he should relate to the younger men and women. He continues from there with counsel regarding care for widows in the church. In verse seventeen he expresses concern about the elders receiving appropriate remuneration. And finally, in verse twenty-three, Paul expresses his concern for Timothy's physical well-being by advising him to use a little wine for the sake of his stomach and his frequent ailments.

Pastoral concern can also be prompted by relational problems in the church – as we see in Paul's admonition to a couple of Philippian church members, Euodia and Syntyche, to *'live in harmony in the Lord.'*[20] In other words, stop fighting and get your relationship back in order.

Because of the nature of their calling, apostles are very involved with planting churches and establishing functioning structures, but they also feel deeply about the quality of care and relational life that exists in each community. In many ways they are trans-local shepherds.

## He built on a strong faith and grace foundation

Paul lays it out so simply and yet so profoundly in Ephesians 2:8:

> *'For by grace you have been saved through faith.'*

In other words, we are saved through faith in the grace of God – or to use a phrase coined by John Piper in one of his excellent books, we are saved by *'faith in future grace.'*[21]

Paul begins and ends all thirteen epistles with a faith blessing of 'future grace' to all those who read his letters. He not only taught about faith, he also ministered faith by boldly declaring promises of God's *future* grace (that is, the grace that is available to us from this point onward into the future), as we see in these examples:

> *'For I am confident of this very thing, that he who began a good work in you will perfect it until the day of Jesus Christ.'* (Philippians 1:6)

*'And my God shall supply all your needs according to his riches in glory in Christ Jesus.'* (Philippians 4:19)

*'Now may the God of peace himself sanctify you entirely; and may your spirit and soul and body be preserved complete, without blame at the coming of our Lord Jesus Christ. Faithful is he who calls you and he also will bring it to pass.'*

(1 Thessalonians 5:23–24)

*'And the God of peace will soon crush Satan under your feet.'* (Romans 16:20)

Paul went to great lengths in his letters to establish the doctrines of faith and grace. In part this was necessary to counter the false teaching that a person could be made righteous by the works of the law. To the church in Rome he writes:

*'Therefore having been justified by faith, we have peace with God through our Lord Jesus Christ, through whom also we have obtained our introduction into his grace in which we stand; and we exult in hope of the glory of God.'* (Romans 5:1–2)

To the Galatian believers who were even more suscept-ible to this legalistic heresy, Paul wrote:

*'[K]now that a man is not justified by observing the law, but by faith in Jesus Christ. So we, too, have put our faith in Christ Jesus that we may be justified by faith in Christ and not by observing the law, because by observing the law no one will be justified.'*

(Galatians 2:16)

The problem for us as evangelicals today is our failure

to understand that the faith that justifies is also the faith that sanctifies. We preach that we are saved 'by grace through faith', but then, by the way we incorporate man-made rules and personal experience in our subsequent exhortation, people are left with the impression that they are sanctified by their own will and works. Paul calls that 'another gospel'. John Piper said that the aim of his book *Future Grace* was

> 'to examine how faith, which is alone the means through which *pardoning grace* justifies, is also the faith through which *empowering grace* sanctifies.' [22]

Paul was so passionate in his preaching on faith in Christ's free grace that some Christians got the idea that the more they sinned, the more opportunity they gave for God to extend his grace toward them.[23] A true 20th century apostle will want to shout it from the house-tops that Christ has become to us not only righteousness but also sanctification.[24] Whether we receive the righteousness of Christ by *imputation* – as we do for our justification – or by *impartation* – for our sanctification, it is always on the basis of 'grace through faith'.

## He built with priestly prayer

Imagine having a spiritual mentor who could say with absolute integrity, *'I constantly remember you in my prayers night and day.'*[25] Or try to visualise receiving a letter from someone you have never met before who tells you what Paul told the Christians in Rome:

> *'God, whom I serve with my whole heart in preaching the gospel of his Son, is my witness how constantly I remember you in my prayers at all times; and I pray*

*that now at last by God's will the way may be opened
for me to come to you.'*                    (Romans 1:9–10)

Paul told everyone to whom he sent letters (with the
exception of Titus) that he prayed for them. And when
Paul prayed for a church, we can be sure that the prayers
were not insignificant or lacking substance. Here, for
example is part of an apostolic prayer offered on behalf
of the believers in Ephesus:

> *'I keep asking that the God of our Lord Jesus Christ,
> the glorious Father, may give you the Spirit of wisdom
> and revelation, so that you may know him better. I
> pray also that the eyes of your heart may be enlight-
> ened in order that you may know the hope to which he
> has called you, the riches of his glorious inheritance in
> the saints.'*                    (Ephesians 1:17–19)

Paul thought big thoughts and served a big God – and
as a result, prayed big prayers!

## He built with servanthood and sacrifice

Throughout in his life, Paul taught by word and deed that
servanthood and sacrifice are foundational to godly
leadership. After describing some of the things he had
been through on behalf of the saints, Paul tells the
Corinthians, *'So death works in us, but life in you'*
(2 Corinthians 4:12). Opposite this verse I have written in
the fly-leaf of my Bible, 'At the point of my death (to self)
is where God's life is released to others.'

To the Thessalonians he wrote:

> *'But we were as gentle among you as a mother feeding
> and caring for her own children. We loved you dearly –*

*so dearly that we gave you not only God's message, but our own lives as well. Don't you remember, dear brothers, how hard we worked among you? Night and day we toiled and sweated to earn enough to live on so that our expenses would not be a burden to anyone there, as we preached God's good news among you.'*

(1 Thessalonians 2:7–9, The Living Bible)

Paul was beaten so many times he lost count; he suffered many imprisonments; he received the dreaded 39 lashes on five occasions; he was beaten with rods three times; he survived stoning; and endured three shipwrecks (on one occasion spending a night and a day in the open sea). His life was constantly at risk. There were dangers from crossing rivers; dangers from robbers; dangers from fellow Jews who plotted against him and Gentiles who considered him a threat; dangers that lay in wait for vulnerable travellers in the city and in the wilderness; and dangers from false brethren.

He laboured and toiled – spiritually, mentally and physically – throughout his ministry life; he suffered exposure to the chilling elements and often went without sleep; many times he was without food and drink.

All this was for the cause of the gospel and the care of the churches – and without any threats of resigning from 'the ministry' if things didn't improve. He understood that for an apostle, position and reputation are nothing, servanthood and sacrifice are everything.

## He built toward discipleship into maturity in Christ

*'And we proclaim him, admonishing every man and teaching every man with all wisdom, that we may*

> *present every man complete* (mature) *in Christ. And*
> *for this purpose also I labour, striving according to his*
> *power, which mightily works within me.'*
>
> (Colossians 1:28)

For Paul, the goal was maturity in Christ; the method, personal discipleship. Jesus said, 'Go and make disciples,' so that was precisely what Paul went ahead and did.

The believers in the early church were usually called *disciples* – as we see in these phrases from Acts chapter 14: '... *the disciples stood around him* ... *after they had preached the gospel to that city and had made many disciples* ... *strengthening the souls of the disciples* ... *they spent a long time with the disciples*...' and so on.

These days we generally use the term *member* instead of *disciple*. The problem with *member* is that it suggests a somewhat passive state of belonging, whereas *disciple* carries the sense of active following and learning. Maybe the reason we 'egalitarian' 20th century Christians prefer not to use the word *disciple* is because the word also suggests subordination, inequality and hierarchy – concepts which are currently out of fashion (except perhaps in the army).

Paul evidently had no qualms about inviting the believers in Corinth, Philippi and Thessalonika to follow him, as we see in these excerpts from his letters to them:

> *'I exhort you therefore, be imitators of me.'*
>
> (1 Corinthians 4:16)

> *'The things you have learned and received and heard and seen in me, practise these things; and the God of peace shall be with you.'* (Philippians 4:9)

> *'You also became imitators of us and of the Lord...'*
>
> (1 Thessalonians 1:6)

I am writing this portion of the book in Buenos Aires, Argentina. Together with ten other leaders from Canada and the United Kingdom, I am a guest of an Assemblies of God church called *Rey de Reyes* (King of Kings). We came here because we were concerned about the spiritual state of young people in many of our family of churches, and because we had received a number of intriguing letters from Abby, a young lady from Oxfordshire Community Churches, who is spending a year in Buenos Aires and has linked up with the *Rey de Reyes* church led by Claudio Freidzon. The following is a portion of one of her letters that grabbed my attention and irresistibly drew me to this city. She writes:

'Firstly, I want to talk about the young people in the church. There are around 1,000 of them – mostly converts, some from the streets or difficult backgrounds – aged between 13 and 25. But they are so different from our youth that at first they seemed unreal. I especially remember those from my encounter with SAS (the name of the youth group back home in England): many seemed quite screwed up, confused, unsure of their faith, and – from the ages of 13–18 particularly – more interested in the material world than the spiritual world.

I assumed this was normal. But even the 10–12's (in the Rey de Reyes church) seemed more in tune with the Spirit than I was when I arrived here. There are no half-hearted Christians; all of them have given themselves 100% over to God. I noticed no bitchiness amongst the girls, just love and affection. Nor is there any fussing about appearance, clothes, make-up, etc.

The relationship between boys and girls is beautiful too: everyone is friends with everyone else.

Nobody is looked down upon or seen as less important because of age. That is why such a large age range all meet together – so that all can benefit from the qualities of each other. Pastor Claudio particularly wanted to share with me some of the teaching they give their youth, and I began to see why there is such a difference. Not at first, though: I openly disagreed with him on some issues until he explained them further, but really the only explanation was when he asked me if they looked happy. That was the only evidence required to convince me the teaching was right and that it worked.

The basic idea is this: to renounce everything from the world and live a life totally ruled by God, with the help and guidance of the Holy Spirit. It is not acceptable to try to compromise with God. We cannot keep one foot in the world and also share fully in God's blessing.

There is no Christian education in Buenos Aires so everybody goes to secular schools. That is really the only contact they have with sin and temptation that they face by themselves. All of them still have non-Christian friends, but they spend time with them on neutral or home territory so that they don't open themselves to difficult situations and temptations. They don't go to discos, nightclubs, bars or places like that – as would be typical of young people in Argentina from a very early age. Nobody drinks except for a glass of champagne at a wedding, nor do any of them want to. Instead, they get "drunk" in church about five times a week on God's "new wine", the Holy Spirit. It's great: no hangover, no cost, no doing things you regret in the morning; just continual blessing.

Young people here spend most of their free time working on God's chosen ministry for their lives. The church believes that God has a special area for each person to use his or her giftings, and actively organises these groups to work within the community. For some, it's working in the slums or the streets or the orphanages. It may be evangelism, leadership, music, teaching, or Bible study, but **everyone** is in a group, under an instructor. Each person also has a "shepherd" figure to talk and pray with. The devotion of these leaders to their charges is wonderful, really loving. There is also a youth pastor who looks after their needs as a whole and in relation to the rest of the church.

It was the teaching about relationships that bothered me at first. Boys and girls, within the rules of the church, aren't allowed to start dating until they are 18! Then, if two people like each other, they must pray, separately and alone, for three months before going together and declaring it to the youth pastor. Then they are allowed to spend time praying together for another 3 months before they go places together. From the day they are 18 they begin to pray for a future partner.

I was horrified and asked why they had to leap straight into a serious relationship. Surely experience should be valued too! The girls I spoke to answered that experience in relationships (and worldly things generally) only led to pain, sin and temptation. In these conditions the Holy Spirit cannot work. I now began to understand (and noticed that everyone is happy with this arrangement).

What it means is that members of the opposite sex are friends and not constantly trying to impress each other. Although they don't question these rules

(I felt like an anarchist when making these enquiries!) they are not dumb sheep, willing to be led anywhere. They are all wonderful, exciting, vibrant human beings – but energetic for God, not for material pleasures. All the effort that could be spent arguing and rebelling is channelled into God, and I've never before seen a group of such happy, joyous young people.

Nor do they listen to non-Christian music. When I vocally disagreed with this idea, they pointed out that most music is written for the glory of those writing it or for money, and not for the glory of God. Individual artists or members of bands often use drugs, abuse alcohol, and have frequent sex outside of marriage – and put these ideas into their songs, however subtly. In these things the Holy Spirit is not present; therefore when we listen to the music it is a time when the Spirit of God has to leave us, and so we are open to attack from evil spirits.

Everyone is discipled!'

I decided to include this rather lengthy excerpt for several reasons: It is an excellent 'eye-witness' report (from a non-leadership perspective) of what God is doing in Argentina, and while we may not adopt every policy and procedure described, there is much we can learn from this dynamic church. Also, it represents a practical, contemporary illustration of the principles of *discipleship*. I have believed in and practised discipleship since 1971. But sad to say, in too many cases, what began in the Spirit degenerated into being maintained in the flesh. Three points are worth mentioning in regard to our experience:

**Firstly**, we strayed from the principle of people being discipled into Christ through the authority of the

Scriptures. In a number of instances, man's authority replaced the authority of Scripture.

**Secondly**, there were some cases involving abuse of authority which drew concern and justifiable criticism.

**Thirdly**, there was an accusation that we were a cult (the 1970s was a time rife with cults, including one led by the notorious Jim Jones). This rumour was spread mostly by those who left us after being placed under discipline because of sinful behaviour, but the result was that we over-reacted to these accusations, eventually losing both the dynamic and the practice of one-to-one discipleship.

Thus it was of particular interest to see discipleship in action in Buenos Aires – some 25 years after we took our fledgling steps in that direction in the UK (and later Canada). Here are some of my notes from that eventful time at *Rey de Reyes* church:

> 'Yesterday evening we attended their Monday "youth night" which is for the purpose of discipling. In attendance were approximately 1,000 young people from 13–25 years of age. The 13–17's met from 6:30 pm to 8:30 pm, then the 18–25–year-olds met from 8:30 pm to 10:30 pm. Both groups started with praise and worship which lasted about thirty minutes, after which they divided into groups of twelve for the purpose of discipling. In this discipling, the Scriptures were the basis and yardstick of their discussions. Tonight we are going along to another discipling meeting which is for the men of the church. Tomorrow, all the women of the church will gather for their discipling programme. The groups are separated according to people's age and spiritual maturity. Each disciple is carefully taken through a handbook which is rooted in the Scriptures and is divided into three sections:

One of the things that has impressed us the most is the spirit of unity that exists amongst these disciples. Those who sit at the back of the packed church building are as enthusiastically involved as those in the front rows. From the cradle to the grave, everyone is being discipled. And just in case anyone has the idea that all these people do is attend meetings, it should be noted that the church has a powerful ministry amongst the city's street kids, resulting in hundreds of them coming to Christ and in turn being discipled in the Monday night classes. Medical and dental help is given freely to the poor, along with clothing and other humanitarian aid.

We asked Claudio Freidzon if there were other evangelical churches in Argentina which practised discipleship. "They all do," he replied, "every one of them; it's normal." '

I fully expect the apostle Paul would have considered discipleship to be the norm as well, since he built in such a way as to encourage growth and maturity by this means. Let me close this chapter with one more way in which Paul built.

## He built 'dangerously'

By saying Paul built dangerously, I am saying that he took risks. Timothy was still a young man when Paul entrusted him with great responsibility. He was left in charge of the church at Ephesus which numbered many thousands. Then Paul sent him to Corinth to remind them of his ways in Christ. This was another large church

– with even more members than Ephesus, and with many more problems. (And remember, there was no opportunity to pick up the phone and have a quick chat with the boss!)

Much more could be said about this dimension of Paul's apostolic building, but suffice it to say that he followed the clear lead of the Chief Apostle, Jesus Christ, who also took the 'risk' of entrusting eternal matters to young men who were often uneducated and unprofessional, but who were teachable and had a heart for the kingdom of God.

As I close this chapter, I would ask you this question: Wouldn't you like to see churches – right across this nation – with the quality of life we have been examining in this chapter?

Well, it is possible, but it will cost you.

How much? you may ask. The answer is very clear: the cost is the discarding of your old 'wineskin' and the risky development of a new one which will include apostles, prophets and evangelists to go alongside of, and in front of, the pastors and teachers you already have. The rest of this book is for those who are willing to take that risk.

### Footnotes

[1] Ephesians 1:10.
[2] Paul refers to this type of 'false apostle' in 2 Corinthians chapter 11.
[3] 1 Corinthians 2:2 and Philippians 1:21.
[4] Hebrews 11:2.
[5] One of the most influential Christian writers of the 20th century, Francis Schaeffer, sounded the alarm on this issue in his book *The Great Evangelical Disaster* (Westchester, Ill.: Crossway Books, 1984).
[6] Ephesians 5:22.
[7] We find an exception to this rule among the early Christians: the Jewish converts at Berea daily examined the Scriptures to see whether the apostle Paul's teachings were in fact true (Acts 16:11).
[8] Romans 1:16.
[9] Or *tutors* (NASB), or *instructors* (KJV).

[10] Eugene H. Peterson, trans. *The Message: The New Testament in Contemporary Language* (Colorado Springs: Navpress, 1993).

[11] F.F. Bruce, *The Pauline Circle* (Paternoster Press, 1995), p. 8.

[12] Ephesians 2:19–22.

[13] A *living* is an Anglican euphemism for the job of a vicar.

[14] Galatians 3:5.

[15] 2 Corinthians 12:12.

[16] The Belgian Congo was the former name of Zaire. See also references to W.F.P. Burton in the *Introduction*.

[17] Acts 13:1 includes Paul in a list of prophets and teachers.

[18] Philemon verse 12.

[19] See Acts 14:23 and Titus 1:5.

[20] Philippians 4:2.

[21] John Piper, *Future Grace* (Sisters, Oregon: Multnomah Books, 1995).

[22] *Ibid.*, p. 21.

[23] Romans 6:1.

[24] 1 Corinthians 1:30.

[25] 2 Timothy 1:3.

# Chapter 4

## Apostles are a Gift from Jesus

Ephesians chapter 4 tells us that the Lord Jesus gave gifts to the church, and that one of these gifts is apostles. In this chapter, I want to focus on *how* apostles are a gift to the church, and how local church elders in particular can benefit from their ministry. The following list represents sixteen ways in which apostles can help a church grow to maturity and assist elders in their governmental responsibilities.

### 1. Apostles help ensure that new churches are planted on solid foundations

Many new churches are planted as an extension of a 'mother' church. Understandably, they are known as 'daughter' churches and as a result, feel somewhat inferior ('tied to mother's apron strings' – especially if financial support is involved). Not only that, but they tend to carry over into the new work many of the weak traits of the mother church. In the New Testament, however, the pattern is different: it was the *apostle* who planted the churches – often with the financial support of sending churches – rather than 'mother' churches planting out and holding authority over other churches.

Apostles think architecturally: they are builders, super-naturally gifted in putting people's lives and ministries together so that they are formed into a cohesive, vibrant, balanced community. With the help of the prophet, they build creatively and are not afraid to demolish an old, unproductive structure, replacing it with one that is more effective and purposeful.

Many local leaders are inclined towards erecting buildings (or figuratively speaking, *temples*). They even reverentially refer to them as 'the house of God'. Apostles, on the other hand, prefer the idea of *tabernacles*, and like to call them 'church facilities'. (I trust the reader will not be too offended with me for those comments, because even though I am talking in generalities, much of this, sadly, is the true situation.)

## 2. Apostles save us from taking short cuts in appointing new elders

Some people get quite worried at the thought of someone from outside the local church being involved in the selection of elders. They are afraid that someone unsuitable might be foisted upon them, but they probably do not understand the way it works. What normally happens is this: local elders may come up with three or four men as possibilities but, through the process of asking the necessary 'awkward' questions, that number, more often than not, gets reduced to one or two.

When I am consulted over the appointment of a new elder, there are a number of questions that I always take the opportunity of asking, such as:

**Does this person act in a priestly way toward the Lord?** In other words, is he a worshipper? Is he a 'player' or just a spectator? To have someone occupying a leadership position who seldom opens his mouth or raises his hands in adoration or prayer to God is presenting a negative role model before the church: it sends out the wrong signals.

**Is this person living a holy life?** Does his character match his gifting?

**Does this person live prudently?** Is he sensitive to the fact that younger Christians are going to be influenced by how he conducts himself, or does he feel compelled to flaunt his freedom at every opportunity? For example, I cannot see anywhere in Scripture where the drinking of wine is forbidden. (I know some of my teetotal friends disagree with me on this point.) However, having said that, I don't believe I should try to make a point of it by 'flaunting' my freedom. In fact, Paul made it clear that my freedom to eat and drink that which others find question-able has nothing whatsoever to do with the kingdom of God.[1] Pursuing my freedom to another's detriment is the opposite of 'seeking first his kingdom and his righteous-ness.'

**Does this person walk openly with those close to him, or does he 'play his cards close to his chest'?** 'Yes-men' do not make good elders – in part because they tend to conceal their true feelings, and when conflicts or disagreements arise, they are likely to shift their allegiance. When that happens, they often start coughing up all manner of past offences and doubts that they have been harbouring for years. Never disqualify a man because of his honesty.

**Do you know whether this person has any 'skeletons in his closet' in the way of unconfessed sin or sexual perver-sions?** Most local elders are too embarrassed to make such enquiries. Brotherly love is a wonderful thing, but it can also contribute to brotherly blindness. Hardly three months go by without me hearing of another elder who has been discovered to be in sin. What is almost worse is hearing that some of these men had struggled with the temptation for years without sharing it with another soul.

**Does he have your 'family genes'?** This question asks whether he has been with you long enough to have imbibed the way you 'keep house' in your church family, and whether he understands and accepts the reasoning that lies behind the way you do things. Conformity without revelation is religious traditionalism – which has been the bane of the church throughout the ages, whereas responses that arise out of understanding and conviction produce lasting fruit.

**Does he have the motivational gift of ruling?** It is one thing to have wisdom and good ideas, and another to carry the authority that comes with 'governmental' grace. For example, if he cannot lead his wife and family properly, you can be certain he will not be able to lead the church adequately. A senior leader once made this shocking comment to me: 'If I were to measure myself against the standards Paul set in order to qualify as an elder, then my failure to lead my wife and children properly would require me to resign from the ministry.'

**Is he an owner or is he a steward?** Has he previously been tested with lesser responsibilities? How did he handle those duties? Did he draw people to himself in a possessive manner, or did he shepherd them with an 'open hand', recognising his role as a steward of the things of God? Is he mature enough to handle the function of serving as an elder to God's people?

**Is he teachable or does he know it all?** If he is not teachable, he probably suffers from a heavy dose of pride or insecurity (or both).

**Does he make it easy for others to bring him correction, or is he manipulative?** For instance, does he try to turn the tables whenever he is challenged, whereby the confronter ends up feeling the guilty one?

## 3. Apostles save us from making rash decisions

Again, the issue of apostles asking the 'awkward' questions is relevant here. Here are some examples:

- *Did you get this from the Lord, or is it just a good idea?*
- *Where is the money going to come from?*
- *And where are you going to get the time to handle this fresh challenge?*
- *What does your wife think?*
- *Is this the right time?*
- *Are you willing to lay this vision down and let the Lord resurrect it? This will verify whether you have heard accurately from God.*

It often turns out that the vision being shared by an individual is authentic, but that the timing is wrong. Proverbs 19:2 says that *'he who makes haste with his feet errs.'*

## 4. Apostles keep us from trying to fit square pegs into round holes

Ministry vacancies in the church are often filled on the basis of who is available and doesn't have too many things to do. But God's strategy for accomplishing the work of the ministry is to distribute the appropriate measures of divine grace (ability) to his carefully selected workers, enabling them to complete successfully each assignment in *his* expertise, strength and wisdom. If we could liken God to a building-site manager, it would be the equivalent of him assigning a plumber to do the plumbing, an electrician to do the electrical wiring, and a bricklayer to lay the bricks.

But what do we do in the building of God's house? Too often we ask plumbers to take care of the electrical work, and electricians to be responsible for the plumbing. If we ask a prophet to fill a pastoral position – a task for which God hasn't given him grace – what does he use to fulfil that ministry? It can be only his own (human) wisdom and ability. In other words, he will be trying to do spiritual work with human resources. Forgive me for trying to explain it in such simplistic terms but, in many situations I am aware of, there is a dire need for structural change (and such change is what apostles are uniquely gifted to help bring about). It is time for us to repent of trying to do the Lord's work in our own wisdom and strength, and to adopt *his* ways and means.

## 5. Apostles can save us from 'wearing out the saints' with unnecessary activity

As my good friend Gerald Coates likes to point out, Jesus didn't say, 'I am come that you might have meetings and have them more abundantly,' but rather that we might have '*life* more abundantly.' Far too many meetings are unnecessary, unproductive, and lacking in purpose and goals. They even can be a substitute for vital kingdom business.

We also need to ask the question, 'Does everyone have to be at every meeting?' This problem of over-activity is particularly relevant as we approach the 21st century. With the decline of physical labour and the breathtaking rise of computer technology, middle management is having ever increasing demands placed upon it. Many of our most effective leaders are in this middle management bracket and are struggling to keep up with the demands on their time.

I know of one such leader who is an elder, a home-group leader and a Bible teacher. He leaves for his place of employment at 7:00 am and returns home at 7:30 pm.

Most nights, he grabs a quick bite to eat and then rushes off to some meeting or other – an elders' meeting, a training night for the home-group leaders – or he may have to visit someone who needs counselling. If senior church leaders fail to take into account the stresses of this type of lifestyle, we will end up contributing to the early demise of some wonderful, committed leaders, and that would be a tragic loss to the body of Christ.

Allow me to give you an example from my own family: Our daughter Rachel and her husband Jeremy have two young children. Together they lead a home group as well as the Sunday School. That in itself is a 'full load', but my son-in-law's job often requires him to work until midnight. And Rachel spends most Friday and Saturday nights with other young women from the church doing outreach – taking tea, coffee and hot rolls to the prostitutes who work the streets in the neighbourhood. Added to this, she has responsibility for a group of dancers who participate in special worship celebrations. I regularly pray that they would be protected from taking on more than they can physically, emotionally or spiritually handle.

## 6. Apostles help us maintain a balanced diet of sound doctrine

Rarely do I find the elders of a church acknowledge that they are failing to feed God's people 'the full council of God', yet seldom do I find a church that is providing quality ministry of the Word on a consistent basis. For example, in some churches there is hardly any teaching on the second coming of Christ: the leaders have neither heard such a message, nor – perhaps in a misguided attempt to avoid controversy – taught on the subject themselves. And if the existence of hell (or heaven for that matter) depended on the subject being raised in some of our evangelical churches, one could be forgiven for thinking that no such place existed!

Whatever happened to good, expository Bible teaching that sowed understanding and deep appreciation for the Word of God? Where is the place provided for those anointed devotional messages that would send you home so in love with Jesus that you thought your heart was going to burst?

With these gaps in the area of 'sound doctrine', it is small wonder that our praise and worship songs may have more to do with *us* and how we are feeling, than with Jesus and what he has done. Thank God for the Graham Kendricks, the Noel Richards, the Chris Bowaters, the Dave Fellinghams, and others whose songs, generally speaking, have theological substance, a Godward focus, and memorable, easy-to-sing melodies. Unfortunately, there are too many songs of the other type – mushy, self-oriented, almost tuneless and needing a heavy beat in order to make the song carry. My conviction is this: our songs are a reflection of our preaching, and until that changes, we cannot expect our songwriters to be inspired with words and melodies that worship and exalt a transcendent God.

## 7. Apostles help us to maintain biblical standards of holiness

The last twenty years have seen a major decline in the standards of holiness in our evangelical churches. Recently I was assisting in praying for people who had come forward at the close of a meeting. One young man was weeping uncontrollably, so I went up and put my arm around his shoulders. After weeping for several more minutes he quietened down, which gave me the opportunity to ask if he would like to tell me what was causing him such pain.

'I've lost my boys,' he blurted out, and then broke out again into loud sobbing. The first thought that came to my mind was that his children had perished in an accident of some kind. Again he quietened down long enough for me to ask him if he would like to talk about it.

This was his story: He had been living common-law with a young lady who had become pregnant and had left him soon after. Following this, he had teamed up with another woman, who also became pregnant and bore him a baby boy. After three years of cohabitation, this lady also left him, taking the child with her. So this was what he meant when he said, 'I've lost my boys.'

When I asked him whether he and these two women had been Christians at the time of their common-law relationship, he replied in a matter-of-fact manner, 'Oh yes.' I failed to detect even one small sign that he was aware that he had sinned against a holy God or that he needed to repent.

A few years ago I was asked to help in a case where a Pentecostal pastor was living with another woman during the week and then collecting his wife on the Sunday morning to accompany him to the church service. Eventually he resigned from the church and he and his wife separated. Within a month he was attending another church together with his new common-law wife – a church where the minister not only knew him but was fully aware of the circumstances. I ended up booking an appointment with the district superintendent to make sure *he* was made fully cognisant of the situation.

Where is the fear of the Lord?

There is nothing new under the sun! The Corinthian

leaders were also guilty of tolerating gross sin within their congregation. But in their case, they had an apostle who confronted them and was not afraid to use his apostolic authority, commanding them to deliver the offending party to Satan for the destruction of the flesh.

## 8. Apostles keep us outwardly focused

There is no shortage with regard to the harvest: it is always ripe. There are always plenty of distressed and downcast people. The problem is that we have a serious labour shortage. As Vic Gledhill, a close friend and colleague, describes it (in his own unique way): 'The real problem of the church is not trying to get bums on chairs; it's trying to get bums *off* chairs.' There are more than enough believers to get the job done; our dilemma is that there just aren't enough volunteers. The church continues to focus on itself and major on minors while the rest of the world goes to hell.

We need to understand the basic issue of our mandate on this earth. Jesus said, *'I will build my church...'* (Matthew 16:18). What he commanded *us* to do was to seek first his kingdom (Matthew 6:33). Let me paraphrase what Jesus was saying in these two statements: 'I will get on with building my family; you give yourselves to carrying out the family business.' A great number of leaders seem to have an inadequate understanding of the church and how it relates to the kingdom of God.

I was with a group of leaders, all of whom carried responsibility for large churches. We happened to be discussing the problem of 'burn-out' amongst church members when one of the leaders made this statement: 'I can't see why there should be a problem! We have a Sunday morning service that lasts ninety minutes, a Sunday evening service that is of similar duration, and a mid-week service that takes up about seventy-five minutes of people's time.' Then he challenged us with the question: 'Now, how can anyone get stressed out on that level of commitment?'

All the man could see were three meetings a week! He was seemingly blind to the kingdom 'family business' that some of these people were involved in (or perhaps that others *should* have been involved in).

Apostles don't view church life through those sorts of spectacles. They use terms like *unceasing, night and day, in every place, in all circumstances*. They see the church not as a place we escape to, but as a community of people who seek first the kingdom of God in their daily lives, who live in the real world and are friends with sinners.

## 9. Apostles help to prevent divisions

One of Satan's main activities is to create pockets of infectious disagreement – especially amongst leaders – in order to keep the saints preoccupied with internal hassles, thereby preventing them from their real task of seeking the kingdom of God. Paul had something to say to each church about avoiding tensions with one another:

> *'Never pay back evil for evil to anyone ... If possible, so far as it depends on you, be at peace with all men.'*
> (Romans 12:17–18)

> *'For I am afraid that perhaps when I come I may find you to be not what I wish ... that perhaps there may be strife, jealousy, angry tempers, disputes, slanders, gossip, arrogance and disturbances.'*
> (2 Corinthians 12:20)

> *'Let us not become boastful, challenging one another, envying one another.'* (Galatians 5:26)

It is true that Paul had disputes with Barnabas and Peter, but one was over the need to safeguard the mission of taking the gospel to the Gentiles, while the other had to do with Paul defending the purity of the gospel. Overall, he demonstrated great patience and forbearance in situations of potential or actual conflict – which is what we would expect of someone in an apostolic role. Basically, apostles will not tolerate divisions that have pride, arrogance, gossip, jealousy and vested interests at their centre.

## 10. Apostles challenge us to have a prophetic vision

A genuine prophetic vision has tremendous power: it touches us in the depths of our being and gnaws away at our insides; it focuses our attention; it produces singleness of purpose; it aligns the saints; it harnesses untapped resources; it obliterates festering aggravations; it motivates people to action.

While prophets are an essential part of prophetic vision in the church, apostles have been gifted by God to help us to:

- *Define the vision.*
- *Prepare for its implementation.*
- *Divide it up into its various components, defining the vision for each part.*
- *Carefully select those who should govern each part (not leaving it to volunteers).*
- *Initiate and organise the training and preparation of new leaders for the future. (As someone has said, 'The future belongs to those who have prepared for it.')*

As a step in this direction, I have sent out a letter to our family of churches, asking the leadership to respond to the following questions:

- *What is your vision for evangelism?*
- *Who is presently in charge of evangelism?*
- *Who do you see will be in charge of it five years from now?*
- *What are you doing in the present to prepare that person for that task?*

The same questions were asked concerning the teaching of Scripture; prayer; house groups; pastoral care; prophetic ministry; ministry to children, youth, senior citizens, the poor; and the leading of praise and worship. Everyone who talked to me about my letter expressed genuine gratitude for it. However, it was only those who submitted the questions (and the issues raised by them) to those in apostolic authority who gained lasting benefit from this exercise.

The sad thing for me in writing this book is knowing that even though some leaders will say, 'This book is really helpful,' nothing will change in their church situation *unless* they themselves have the gifting of an apostle, or they open up their church family to receive apostolic input. In that sense, reading this book could actually be an inoculation against the real thing.

## 11. Apostles help us to build governmentally

It seems from the evidence of Scripture that every church planted by Paul and his apostolic team was soon set up with a government of elders, and that it was apostles who set these elders in place. In Acts 14:23 we read, '...*and when they had appointed elders in every church*...' The Greek word translated *appoint* means to decide by the pointing or lifting of the hand. Some Bible scholars suggest that the local believers were the ones who democratically decided who the elders were to be. But this cannot be substantiated from this verse because the word *appoint* is describing the action taken by Paul and Barnabas, not an action by the local church.

Paul expected elders to lead, to rule, and to be over the flock. Some Bible teachers like to say that leaders are *alongside* the flock. Well, this may be true, but leaders also *have charge over* the flock according to 1 Thessalonians 5:12.

Paul modelled church government according to the way he himself exercised authority. For example, when he wrote to Philemon concerning Onesimus being received back, he expected his request to be obeyed (Philemon verse 21). He spoke about the authority he had in Christ (2 Corinthians 10:8, 13:10). He reminds the church of the commandments he gave them by the authority of the Lord Jesus (1 Thessalonians 4:2).

When Paul sent other leaders to teach and act on his behalf – such as Timothy and Epaphroditus – he expected them to be received fully by the local church as if they were receiving him. And he gave very clear instructions to the churches, such as ordering the Corinthians to excommunicate a man who was committing incest, and warning them against using the secular law courts when they should have brought their disputes to some wise, believing men in the church.

Jesus taught that leadership should be provided within a framework of servanthood and humility, but that in no way diminishes the necessary governmental role carried by leaders – as we see throughout the pages of the New Testament.

## 12. Apostles help you to be disciplined in delegating responsibilities

Too many leaders believe that they cannot afford the time to delegate responsibilities to others. The truth is, they cannot afford *not* to. They fail to understand that their physical, emotional and spiritual health is at stake – not to mention the long-term spiritual health of the congregation. Doing it all oneself may be a short-term gain, but very soon the 'one man ministry' ends up becoming a serious long-term loss. The words of Jethro to Moses still apply:

> *'You will surely wear out, both yourself and these people who are with you, for the task is too heavy for you; you cannot do it alone.'*          (Exodus 18:18)

## 13. Apostles help you to guard the spiritual environment of the community

It is frighteningly easy for local elders to allow the spiritual level of a church to decline to the point where one no longer senses the manifest presence of the Lord. Churches with no vision are particularly vulnerable to such decline, which may begin with apathy and self-indulgence, and end with hidden sin, unforgiveness, prayerlessness and disobedience.

> *'Where there is no vision, the people are un-restrained...'*          (Proverbs 29:18)

Or as my highly-esteemed friend Dennis Peacocke says,

> 'The natural state of the garden is weeds, not flowers.'

I have been amazed to see how far the spiritual state of a church can decline before its elders wake up to the seriousness of their plight. Elders who fail to keep on spiritual alert with regard to the care, protection and holiness of those allotted to their charge are guilty of a dereliction of duty. In the First World War, a soldier found guilty of falling asleep on guard duty was given the death sentence. That sounds harsh, but the same principle can be found in Ezekiel 33:1–9 where the Lord outlines the duty of a watchman and the awesome responsibility that goes with it.

## 14. Apostles help you to confront your problems

Someone has said that the great scourge of leaders is unresolved problems. Being a good leader does not guarantee the absence of trouble. In fact, we have a promise from Jesus that guarantees the opposite:

> *'In this world you will have trouble.'*　　　(John 16:33)

A good leader willingly accepts that trouble is inevitable, but what makes him stand out from the rest is his ability to confront and resolve problems.

Procrastination is a leader's arch enemy. If you are like me, you can tend to allow your correspondence tray to build up. The effect on me is a nagging feeling that says I am not doing a good job. This is a form of anxiety, which, if allowed to continue, will make me feel worn out and a little depressed. Usually I come to my senses in time to prevent any serious depression from taking root, and, in one great flourish of activity, I give myself to clear the backlog. When that is done, the anxious feeling is gone, replaced by a sense of exhilaration that, finally, the job has been finished: it's no longer 'hanging there' somewhere in the background of my mind.

Many unsuccessful leaders spend far too much time fiddling about, attempting to resolve minor matters. In reality, this is a form of escapism. The activity makes them feel they are being gainfully employed, but deep down inside they know they are not doing a good job. What a blessing it is to have an experienced and trusted friend with whom you can spread out the details of a major problem, and who is willing and able to ask you searching questions. Not that he gives you the answers, but he helps you to formulate the right solutions – and, in the case of an apostolic leader, inspires you and spurs you into action.

## 15. Apostles help us to move out in the supernatural and take risks

I have tremendous admiration for men who carry a true shepherd's heart, especially if they also have a teaching gift. As pastor/teachers, they provide the feeding and care that is so essential for a healthy congregation. But I am bound to say that many churches being led by such men rarely seem to take risks in the supernatural, and when they do, they prefer to do so in a corner. That is unlike the pattern given to us by the Great Shepherd, our Lord Jesus Christ:

> '*And Jesus was going about all the cities and the villages, teaching in their synagogues, and proclaiming the gospel of the kingdom, and healing every kind of disease and every kind of sickness. And seeing the multitudes, he felt compassion for them, because they were distressed and downcast like sheep without a shepherd. Then he said to his disciples, "The harvest is plentiful, but the workers are few. Therefore beseech the Lord of the harvest to send out workers into his harvest." And having summoned his twelve disciples, he gave them authority over unclean spirits, to cast*

> *them out, and to heal every kind of disease and every
> kind of sickness.'*                    (Matthew 9:35–10:1)

I have written in my Bible underneath the words *'like
sheep without a shepherd'* the following: 'We cannot
pastor without God's power to heal.' The verses quoted
above make it very clear that for Jesus, healing was a part
of pastoring, and he sent his workers (the disciples) into
the harvest to pastor the same way. It isn't an issue of
signs and wonders for signs-and-wonders' sake: it's a
matter of Jesus feeling compassion for hurting humanity.
From Genesis to Revelation we have clear evidence of a
compassionate, healing God. If we consider ourselves to
be *under-shepherds*, we ought also to be *under-healers*.

## 16. Apostles help us make room for the other Ephesians 4 ministries

Pastors and teachers are not always comfortable having
prophets and evangelists around them – especially
prophets. Prophets never seem to be satisfied with the
status quo. They have a habit of sniffing out hidden
problems (and pastors feel they have enough problems,
thank you very much). They are too direct (undiplomatic)
and decisive (impetuous) for the pastor's liking. And they
are unpredictable. Pastors don't like unplanned interrup-
tions.

Pastors are quite happy to go to a prophetic conference
or even to have the occasional visit from a prophet –
whom they graciously allow to preach to the church (for
a change of pace). But it's the *resident* prophet who stands
out as a problem: he's the one who gets under their skin.

Of course, the resident evangelist is another 'trouble-
maker'. He's never satisfied. Even if you are in the middle

of a massive evangelistic outreach, he will protest, 'It's too little, too late.'

I'm obviously overstating things a little: these differences in motivational gifts have their funny side; however, in everyday church life, they also may result in a lot of friction. The fact is, prophets and evangelists *can* be difficult people, but they are Christ's love-gifts to the church just as much as pastors are.

Furthermore, it is my conviction that until we see the gift of *apostles* restored to the church, we will not see many full-time evangelists or full-time prophets. The problem is: the price is too high. Allow me to show you what I mean. As a speaker at a leaders' seminar, I was approached by a thirty-five year old pastor who asked for my advice concerning the release of evangelism in his congregation. He told me that the church had never exceeded seventy members in its seventy-year history, and that most of the time, only fifty people attended on a Sunday.

'Tell me,' I said to him, 'how serious are you about seeing things change?'

'Very!' he enthusiastically responded. 'I'm willing to do anything.'

Then I challenged him, 'Well, are you willing to return to secular work and invite an evangelist to come for at least two years to serve in your place, in order to equip the saints to become evangelistic?'

His face fell. After a while he quietly replied, 'I'd have to really think about that.'

I could tell by the look in his eyes that I had asked an impossible price, and I uncharitably thought to myself, *'Well, that's another part of Christ's church locked up by one man's vested interests.'*

If we stop and think about it, isn't it an awful tragedy that many believers are incarcerated in 'pastoral prisons' instead of being released into all the great evangelistic plans that Jesus has for his church? His command hasn't changed: it is still *'Go into all the world...'* I believe Jesus is saying to the leaders of his church, *'Let my people go!'*

Prophets have a wonderful gift of releasing people into their unique destiny in God. But history records that prophets have not fared well at the hands of God's people. Jerusalem – the 'city of peace' – not only rejected God's prophets, it also carried a reputation for stoning them. As a result, Jerusalem lost her place as a 'crown of beauty' and a 'royal diadem', and was instead compared to Hagar and Sodom and Egypt. If Jerusalem was thus judged by God for rejecting the prophets sent to her, could a similar judgement befall the churches that do the same? May we not be found wanting in that awesome day of accountability.

Jesus declared of those he sent, *'He who receives you receives me...'*[2] When we consider that Jesus still sends his messengers to us – in the form of Ephesians 4 ministries – it follows that to reject the one whom he sends is to reject Jesus *himself.* He goes on to say, *'Anyone who receives a prophet because he is a prophet will receive a prophet's reward...'*[3] Let us not miss out on the reward that Jesus wants to give to his people as they receive his prophets.

Apostles see prophets working alongside them in a complementary way,[4] like a knife with a fork. They receive prophets and evangelists as indispensable members of the team. They place confidence in the unpredictable prophet and the larger-than-life evangelist, and as a result, these two ministries are released to the church.

## A concluding word ...

One should not conclude from these sixteen points that

apostles can solve every problem, answer every question, and meet every need. What they can do – and are meant to do – is to serve the body of Christ in a *foundational* role, making room for *all* of the ministries sent by the Lord Jesus, and setting in place that which is necessary for the ongoing health and growth of the church. In light of the fact that apostles are as human as anyone else, we would be unwise to expect the objectives of this chapter to be fully met all of the time. But neither should we under-estimate what God can and will do through his servants when we open up our hearts and our churches to receive them.

### Footnotes

[1]  See Romans chapter 14 and 15:1–3.

[2]  Matthew 10:40 Note that the disciples were relatively untrained in ministry and lacking in certain character qualities when Jesus spoke these words.

[3]  Matthew 10:41 That's complementary, not *complimentary*. Remember, these are prophets.

# Chapter 5

## The Prime Vision of the Apostle

*'To him be glory in the church and in Christ Jesus to all generations for ever and ever. Amen.'*

(Ephesians 3:21)

A true apostle sees the big picture. He is not small-minded or parochial in his thinking. He is neither sectarian nor denominational – but he does think *family*. Dick Benjamin of Abbotts Loop, Alaska puts it very simply:

'An apostle paints with a broad brush.'

Therefore an apostle will recognise that there are borders to the areas of his prime involvement and limits on his time and energy. He is committed to playing his part – however great or small – in seeing the Father glorified in the universal church of Jesus Christ. Although he may be in a denomination, the denomination is not in *him*.

There are at least five truths that control and motivate a true apostle's thinking and activity:

First of all, he believes that God's original purpose in creation was to fill the entire earth with sinless, humble, obedient, God-dependent people who would rule this planet from a position of being under God's authority:

> *'And God blessed them; and God said to them, "Be fruitful and multiply, and fill the earth and subdue it; and rule over the fish of the sea and over the birds of the sky and over every living thing that moves on the earth."'* (Genesis 1:28)

Imagine an earth without pain, sickness, disease, decay or death; a world in which there was no war, no famine, no domestic strife or divorce, no murder, no rape, no robbery – in fact, no crime whatsoever; a society in which there was no greed, no hate, no malice, no selfishness, no rebellion, no pride. This was God's original plan.

But Adam and Eve decided to submit to Satan's temptation, and in so doing, they became his slaves. In Romans 6:16, Paul writes:

> *'Do you not know that when you present yourselves to someone as slaves for obedience, you are slaves of the one whom you obey?"*

Once Adam and Eve became Satan's servants, the 'keys of government' that God had given them were legally snatched away by the devil. In effect, Adam and Eve committed 'high treason' in this act of disobedience.

Redemption is not a man-centred issue (as is so often presented in our pulpits). Redemption is the restoration of God's original plan. That plan, of course, includes our salvation and God's unfailing love for mankind, but we should never lose sight of the truth that at the heart of redemption stands God's glory. And for the glory of his name, God had already devised a plan to legally take back the keys that Adam had so treacherously given away.

God didn't waste any time in declaring to Satan that there would come forth from the woman a child who would crush his head. Satan would be able to 'bruise the heel' of the Redeemer, but it would cost the devil his head – and the authority he had usurped from God's delegated representative. Several thousand years later there came to planet Earth a sinless, humble, obedient Son who ruled from a position of being under his Father's authority. He did not come to do his own will, and his authority was from being under authority:

> *'I can do nothing on my own initiative. As I hear, I judge; and my judgement is just, because I do not seek my own will, but the will of him who sent me.'*

(John 5:30)[1]

Finally, through his death he destroyed Satan who had the power of death[2] – reducing to zero his authority and legal right to accuse – and took back the keys. At the same time, through the death and resurrection of Jesus, a new creation was birthed: a people who have been cleansed from sin, justified and sanctified, who are to fill the whole earth and, under the Lordship of Jesus Christ, seek to carry out the original mandate entrusted to Adam and Eve. That is why our Lord taught us to pray:

> *'Thy kingdom come.*
> *Thy will be done,*
> *On earth as it is in heaven.'*[3]

It is this understanding that keeps an apostle from the pathetically small vision of just filling the pews on a Sunday morning (especially if those pews are occupied by people whose only interest is to be blessed personally and have their needs met). A while ago I received a brochure in the mail advertising a conference for pastors. The theme was: *How to Break the 200 Barrier*. I crumpled the paper into a ball and flung it into the waste paper bin exclaiming, 'Two hundred for what! Two hundred to keep the pews warm on a Sunday morning?' Now if the wording had been, *How to Disciple, Prepare and Send 200 Soldiers to God's Battlefront*, that would have been a different matter. Thank God for organisations such as *Youth With a Mission* and *Operation Mobilisation* which are committed to the training and equipping of young people in order to send them to the nations with the gospel. But the reason such groups exist is because the local church is failing in its God-ordained commission to disciple all nations.

Secondly, an apostle believes there is a particular glory that God receives when his people are living by grace through faith. John Piper puts it this way:

> 'My passion is to assert the supremacy of God in every area of life. My discovery is that God is supreme not where he is simply served with duty but where he is savoured with delight. *"Delight yourself in the Lord"* (Psalm 37:4) is not a secondary suggestion. It is a radical call to pursue your fullest satisfaction in all that God promises to be for you in Jesus. It is a call to live in the joyful freedom and sacrificial love that comes from faith in future grace.' [4]

One of the key statements in this book by John Piper is:

> 'God is most glorified in us when we are most satisfied in him.'

To which I can only say, amen and amen.

Thirdly, the apostle believes that all of God's people are being built together into a dwelling of God in the Holy Spirit. He understands that our bodies are temples of the Holy Spirit[5] and that the whole church is the corporate temple of God.[6] In other words, the corporate temple is made up of individual temples. Many apostles believe that in John 14:2, the phrase *'In my Father's house are many dwelling places,'* means *In my Father's temple there are many temples.* In the following verses, Jesus goes on to say:

> *'[F]or if I go to prepare a place for you, I will come again and receive you to myself; that where I am, there you may be also.'*

The traditional interpretation of that passage is that since Jesus returned to heaven after his death and resurrection, he has been busy building houses for our future occupation. Such theology has spawned little ditties such as 'Build me a little cabin in the corner of glory land.' Do you really think Jesus is in heaven, hammer and nails at the ready, building a home for you? Once again, such theology makes it all man-centred.

For one thing, when Jesus said *'I go to prepare a place for you,'* he was almost certainly using the picture of the Old Testament high priest who once a year entered the Holy of Holies with the blood of the sacrifice for the atonement of Israel's sins. This is described by the writer to the Hebrews:

> *'But when Christ appeared as a high priest of good things to come, he entered through the greater and more perfect tabernacle, not made with hands, that is to say, not of this creation; and not through the blood*

*of goats and calves, but through his own blood, he entered the holy place once for all, having obtained eternal redemption.'* (Hebrews 9:11–12)

In Ephesians 2:13, Paul writes:

*'But now in Christ Jesus you who formerly were far off have been brought near by the blood of Jesus.'*

Jesus has, at the cost of his blood, prepared a place for us – a place where *he* dwells within his corporate temple: a place within the body of Christ. This temple has a present-day dimension – in terms of our placement in the church family (relationally and functionally), and an eternal dimension – since we are also part of what someone has called 'God's *forever* family'. The members of that family can look forward to ongoing relationships and ongoing function throughout eternity. What a wonderful place he prepares for us!

But what does Jesus mean in John 14:3 when he says: *'I will come again and receive you to myself ...?'* Some commentators see this as the second coming of Christ, but the context doesn't seem to point to that interpretation because in verse 18 Jesus says:

*'I will not leave you as orphans, I will come to you. After a little while the world will behold me no more; but you will behold me; because I live you will live also.'*

It seems obvious that Jesus is referring to the period between his resurrection and his ascension. In verse 16 and 17 he refers to the Holy Spirit coming to be with them and to dwell in them. In verse 23 he speaks of the Father and himself coming to make their abode with

those who love him and keep his word. And in Ephesians
2:22, Paul points out that we are being built together in
order that God may indwell us by the Holy Spirit. Notice
that Paul is using the present tense: *are* being built.

In the book of Revelation, however, we see the
completed picture:

> *'And I saw the holy city, new Jerusalem, coming down
> out of heaven from God, made ready as a bride adorned
> for her husband. And I heard a loud voice from the
> throne, saying, "Behold, the tabernacle of God is
> among men, and he shall dwell among them, and they
> shall be his people, and God himself shall be among
> them ... "'*                     (Revelation 21:2–3)

It seems to me that the passage in John 14 and Ephesians 2:13–22 refers to the period of time between the
resurrection and the second coming of Christ, during
which time we have the pledge[7] of the Spirit. But in
Revelation 21 we have the grand consummation of the
eternal purposes of God expressed in the *'measure of the
stature that belongs to the fullness of Christ'* (Ephesians
4:13), the completion of the mystery that had been
*'revealed to the holy apostles and prophets in the Spirit'*
(Ephesians 3:5), and the full manifestation of the triune
God engaged with his redeemed people.

In the meantime, the work of building continues, as we
see in this excerpt from Peter's first letter:

> *'[Y]ou also, as living stones, are being built up as a
> spiritual house for a holy priesthood, to offer up
> spiritual sacrifices acceptable to God through Jesus
> Christ.'*                        (1 Peter 2:5)

Fourthly, the apostle carries God's heart in wanting to

see the Father *'bring many sons to glory'* (Hebrews 2:10). The purpose of the cross with all its suffering and shame was to rescue slaves from the kingdom of Satan and transfer them into the kingdom of his dear Son, and to see them transformed into the likeness of his Son. It is the work of the Father to make us sons, for we read:

> *'For both he who sanctifies* [Jesus] *and those who are sanctified are all from one Father; for which reason he* [Jesus] *is not ashamed to call them brethren...'*
> (Hebrews 2:11)

Evangelism is never far from the mind and concern of a true apostle. The *Great Commission* is also *his* great commission, and whether he is preaching the gospel himself or making room for gifted evangelists to practise their craft makes no difference. Even when some would preach Christ from a wrong motive, he can still find some good in it:

> *'The former preach Christ out of selfish ambition, not sincerely, supposing that they can stir up trouble for me while I am in chains. But what does it matter? The important thing is that in every way, whether from false motives or true, Christ is preached. And because of this I rejoice.'* (Philippians 1:17–18)

Fifthly, apostles have an overriding passion to see the body of Christ come to a place of unity and maturity. The words that Paul wrote to the Ephesian church reverberate in their hearts:

> *'... until we all attain to the unity of the faith, and of the knowledge of the Son of God, to a mature man, to*

> *the measure of the stature which belongs to the fullness*
> *of Christ.'* (Ephesians 4:13)

While God is sovereign and could accomplish this without *any* human involvement, he has chosen to bring about the unity and maturity of the body of Christ by means of the five-fold ministries described in verse 11. These ministries are to train and release each member of the body into the 'kingdom work force', but the sad reality is, there still exists massive unemployment within our church communities, and I believe that will remain so until we see *all* of Christ's equipping gifts recognised and received.

If the training of building site workers was limited to plumbers and electricians, our construction industry would be in a sorry state. Yet, that is the kind of predicament the church is in. There is little use in praying for God to be glorified in his church and in Christ Jesus (as Paul did in his letter to the Ephesians) if we are unwilling or unavailable for God's power to be at work within the church according to the biblical pattern. The building work cannot be done by one man, nor by a large group of men of just one or two types. It takes the *five-fold* ministries – including the primary and pivotal gifts of apostles and prophets – to bring about the kind of church God is wanting to build.

Apostles think in corporate terms, in partnerships. They are delegators. They know the task is too immense for one man to tackle it on his own, so it is perfectly natural for them to form teams. In the next chapter we will examine how apostles face such a challenge.

### Footnotes

[1]  See also John 5:27–27 and Matthew 8:8–9).
[2]  Hebrews 2:14 and Revelation 1:18.
[3]  Matthew 6:10.

4  *Future Grace*, p. 399.
5  1 Corinthians 6:19.
6  1 Corinthians 3:16–17 *'you* (plural) *are a temple...'* See also 2 Corinthians 6:16.
7  Ephesians 1:14; 2 Corinthians 5:5.

# Chapter 6

## Building an Apostolic Team

In reflecting on ministry teams, I have often thought of Billy Graham and the men and women who have worked with him over many years. They are the most focused, envisioned, loyal, faithful team a man could ever wish for – which not only says a lot for the individuals on the team, it also speaks volumes about the quality of the leader.

There must have been a few tense moments that tested their commitment and relationships since the team started to be formed in 1947, but one would never know it from watching them. Billy Graham is an evangelist of the highest anointing, but for many he is also a spiritual father; which brings me to the first thing I want to say about building an apostolic team.

### The leader needs to be an apostolic father

Priests in the Roman Catholic and Anglo-Catholic tradition are addressed as *Father* – a practice which I believe Jesus spoke against when he said:

> *'And do not call anyone on earth "father", for you have one Father, and he is in heaven.'*[1]

However, Paul could say in 1 Corinthians 4:15:

> *'For if you were to have countless tutors in Christ, yet you would not have many fathers; for in Christ Jesus I became your father through the gospel.'*

Clearly, Paul saw a difference between the use of *father* as a title, and the existence of a fathering relationship with people in the church. For instance, he saw no problem in addressing both Timothy and Titus as his true *sons* in the Lord.

It may not be that all apostles are spiritual fathers, but it would seem essential that anyone forming an apostolic team would need to carry the conviction that God had called him to be a father. By the same token, this 'fathering' anointing would need to be recognised by the other members of the team.

## Team members are selected, not volunteers

It is essential that each member of the team be carefully and prayerfully selected. The concept of choosing team members by selecting them (rather than using volunteers or a 'democratic' selection process) may cut across our western mentality, but it is thoroughly biblical. We see an interesting example of this in the life of Moses. First he *volunteered* his services as deliverer – or as Stephen explained it in Acts chapter 8, *'It entered his mind ... and he supposed ... '* In other words, it was just a good idea! And we know what came of that! Forty years later came the burning bush encounter, and a reluctant Moses was appointed (that is, *selected*) by God to bring about Israel's deliverance from Egypt.

The appointment of prophets like Moses and Jeremiah did not involve a third party, but was a direct encounter with Jehovah God. But there are many *other* examples where God made his choice known through human agency: Joshua was chosen by Moses; David was singled-out by Samuel; Elisha was appointed through Elijah; Barnabas chose Saul to help him at Antioch; Paul picked Timothy and later took Silas with him; and – in the case of history's very first apostolic team – the twelve disciples were hand-picked by Jesus:

> *'And he went up to the mountain and summoned those whom he himself wanted and they came to him. And he appointed twelve, that they might be with him, and that he might send them out to preach, and to have author-ity to cast out the demons.'*　　　(Mark 3:13–15)

One point to remember in all of this is that those chosen were 'minding their own business' at the time. Probably the last thing on their minds was the thought of leaving their homes and jobs and quite possibly ending up as martyrs. They didn't ask for the assignment, they were selected!

## Team members must be joined to the apostolic leader

It is absolutely vital that each member of the team has a revelation that God has joined him or her as a functioning joint[2] to the leader. The prevalence of broken covenants, disloyalty, church-hopping and pastor swapping reveals that modern day Christians have precious little under-standing of the body of Christ being comprised of parts (members) which are linked by functioning joints – that is, covenantal working relationships.

Once a believer sees this truth, his options are greatly diminished: the 'back door' is no longer seen as a credible alternative. He is 'trapped' by his revelation, much like the disciples who may have felt like leaving Jesus at times, but had run out of options: *'Lord, to whom shall we go?'* Peter asked rhetorically, *'You have the words of eternal life.'*

You can be certain that Cliff Barrows knows that God joined him to Billy Graham; similarly, George Beverly Shea. It is in part because of this unity that the Billy Graham crusades are such a formidable evangelistic force. One thing I am careful to ascertain concerning a potential team member is whether he or she has a history of broken relationships. If that is the history, the chances are the same thing will happen again. It was possibly this factor that led Paul to conclude that he could not afford to include John Mark on the team for his second apostolic mission.

## Team members must be 'team players'

Each member must be a team player and have a revelation that God has joined him or her to the rest of the team. You can imagine the problems if a member related well to the leader but wouldn't receive the other members of the team – especially if he saw himself as superior to them. I have experienced such a situation on at least three occasions, and am thankful that they all came to the necessary (but sad) conclusion: those persons left us.

An even worse scenario is when a member believes God has joined him or her to the other members of the team but not to the leader. Any team member who thinks such a situation can remain unresolved is greatly deluded. Jesus said:

> *'Whoever is not with me is against me; and he who does not gather with me scatters.'*[3]

## The importance of family genes

Just as each natural family has its own unique characteristics, so it is in the spiritual family. Thus the members of
an apostolic team all need to have a revelation of their
spiritual 'family genes'. When Paul sent Timothy to
Corinth, he could confidently say to the church, *'He will
remind you of my way of life in Christ Jesus, which agrees
with what I teach everywhere in every church.'*[4] To the
Philippians, Paul could testify that Timothy was *'of
kindred spirit.'*[5]

In some denominations, a young person, after complet-
ing his Bible college training, is immediately posted to a
different congregation and given leadership responsibility
– often as youth pastor. In many cases tensions develop
over doctrinal differences, incompatible standards or
contrasting styles. And sometimes the situation deterior-
ates to the point where a church split is unavoidable. The
problem: there is a clash of family genes.

Let me give you an example that many pastors in the
UK and North America would find familiar. *Youth With
a Mission* is one of my favourite church organisations.
They do a good job of discipling the young people who
join their ranks. The problem starts when these young
people, having taken on *Youth With a Mission* genes,
return to their home church. At that point, they often find
it difficult to fit back in to the old ways – to integrate
successfully into the existing structure – which then may
result in tension, competing vision, or even a parting of
ways. As a result, *Youth With a Mission* receives bad
publicity – which is both unfortunate and unfair.

## The authority of the leader

Each member must be willing to submit to the authority of

the leader in all team matters. You cannot have two sets of hands on the steering wheel without trouble occurring. That is in fact what happened to Paul and Barnabas when they sharply disagreed over whether John Mark should go with them on their second apostolic mission. John Mark had deserted them at Pamphylia (Acts 13:13) and, as mentioned previously, it would seem that Paul was unable to trust the young man sufficiently a second time.

Whether John Mark turned back because the leadership of the team had shifted from his cousin Barnabas to Paul is something about which we can only speculate. However, it is worth noting that Luke (a meticulous writer) recorded the following: that it was Paul – not Barnabas – who was filled with the Spirit and took authority in dealing with Elymas the magician (Acts 13:9), and that when the team put out to sea from Paphos, it was *'Paul and his companions'* (verse 13) – Barnabas is not mentioned.

No one likes the thought of being led by a dictator, and that is not what the Bible teaches. But neither do the Scriptures support the democratic model for church government. The pattern that we see in the pages of the New Testament is one of consultative leadership, where maximum room is given for discussion, dialogue and input, but the final decision rests with leadership. We see this demonstrated in the Council of Jerusalem (Acts 15) where much discussion and consultation (not to mention heated debate) ensued over the place of the law and circumcision in the lives of Gentile believers. In the end, James stood up and brought the judgement – with which they all agreed – and peace was restored to the church.

## The place of young people

Apostolic teams should include young people. I find it

fascinating to observe the place God gave young people in both Old and New Testament times. For instance, we have young Samuel whose prophetic words were so accurate the Bible says not one of them *'fell to the ground.'*[6] Then there is David who was so young that his father didn't even consider it worth recalling him from the fields to stand with his brothers before Samuel. Jeremiah was perhaps as young as twelve years old when God appointed him to be a prophet to the nations.[7] And Joash was only seven years old when he became king![8]

But it is Paul's choosing of Timothy that I find so challenging. There can be little doubt that Paul was taking a real risk when he left him at Ephesus to lead the church there apostolically: as previously mentioned, this church numbered several thousand. Paul instructed him to deal with those who were teaching strange doctrines and to appoint elders (among many other things). In 1 Timothy 4:11 he says, *'Prescribe and teach these things,'* which means *keep commanding and teaching these things*. No wonder Paul continues in verse 12: *'Let no one look down on your youthfulness.'* If Paul could include a Timothy on his team, we should be willing to do the same.

## The team should include prophets, evangelists, pastors and teachers

Since Jesus saw fit to give a variety of ministries to his church, it follows that wherever possible, each of the Ephesians 4 equipping gifts should be represented on the team. If we want to see a release of evangelists from within the church, it won't be pastors who will be able to equip them. Pastors equip pastors and evangelists equip evangelists; the same principle applies to prophets and teachers.

When we are having our teeth fixed, and the dentist approaches us, drill in hand, saying, 'Now open your mouth wide,' it's reassuring to know that it was another dentist who trained him – and not a plumber or a DIY [9] amateur!

## The importance of vulnerability and full disclosure

For a team member to conceal personal sins or, as the saying goes, hold his cards close to his chest, is detrimental to the whole team. A chain is only as strong as its weakest link, and an apostolic team (or any ministry team for that matter) cannot enjoy true fellowship if its members do not walk in the light.

> *'[I]f we walk in the light as he himself is in the light, we have fellowship with one another, and the blood of Jesus his Son cleanses us from all sin.'*    (1 John 1:7)

> *'Therefore, confess your sins to one another, and pray for one another, so that you may be healed.'*
>
> (James 5:16)

Recently I was approached by a man whom I dearly love and highly regard, asking if he and I could have a chat together over a meal. It was then I learned that some fifteen years earlier, I had treated him uncaringly and dismissively when he had come to me for help. It was a painful discovery, but there was no doubt whatsoever: I was guilty! I immediately acknowledged my wrong and was instantly and graciously forgiven. But as I drove home, I couldn't help asking myself the question: *What was there in me that kept him from confronting me with my sin? And how different things might have been between us if*

*he had been willing at that time to be vulnerable and walk in
the light with me.*

For the rest of my life I am committed to walking
alongside others with full disclosure, and will insist that
all members in my team are willing to do the same.
Watchman Nee once said, 'If I have not apologised to
someone recently, darkness has entered my soul somehow.' I would add the following to the great man's
challenge:

> 'If I am retaining a secret hurt or concern regarding
> another, this also means that "darkness has entered
> my soul somehow."'

It is a most precious gift to be able to look into the eyes of
another whom you love and know that there are no
shadows or question marks between you.


## No 'Nine to Fivers'

You cannot afford to have clock-watchers on your team.
Each member needs to be a faithful, hard worker. When
Paul wrote to the church in Rome, he sent greetings to
Persis, saying, *'Greet Persis the beloved, who has worked
hard in the Lord.'* What a wonderful commendation!

The Bible records that it was usually people who were
busily at work whom God chose to serve him. Moses and
David were shepherding their flocks; Elisha was ploughing with twelve oxen – no mean task, considering the
strength of such a herd; Gideon, despite the lurking
danger of the Midianites, was courageously threshing the
wheat; Peter and Andrew were fishing; and James and
John were mending their nets.

I'm always a little wary of people who think they are
too spiritual to give a helping hand in practical tasks. I

have even heard comments like, 'I get someone else to come and take care of the house; it's more important that I get on with my ministry.' Such people fail to see that they are setting an example which is different from the biblical norm:

> *'Older women likewise are to be reverent in their behaviour, not malicious gossips, not enslaved to much wine, teaching what is good, that they may encourage the young women to love their husbands, to love their children, to be sensible, pure, workers at home, kind, being subject to their own husbands, that the word of God may not be dishonoured.'* (Titus 2:3–5)

In the King's Bible College in Scotland, we are careful to mix the study of God's word with a healthy dose of practical tasks. It has several benefits: it helps keep the costs down, it gives the students a break from intellectual labours, and it teaches them that practical work is also spiritual. The latter is a principle still practised by monastic orders throughout the world – a daily discipline in work, word and prayer.

## The role of persistent, focused energy (zeal)

It's not enough that team members are hard-working. They also need to be zealous for God. Whenever I think of zealous people in the Scriptures, two names always come to mind. The first, of course, is Jesus. In the account of his cleansing the temple by driving out the merchants and money-changers, it is recorded that the disciples remembered that it was written, *'Zeal for your house will consume me.'*[10]

The second person is the prophet Elisha. In 2 Kings chapter 2 we read the story of what happened on the journey leading to Elijah's departure from this earth in a whirlwind. Three times Elijah asks Elisha to stay behind, but three times Elisha answers, *'As the Lord lives, and as you yourself live, I will not leave you.'*

Finally the two of them cross the Jordan and Elisha hears the words he has been waiting for: *'Ask what I shall do for you before I am taken from you.'*

Elisha, fully aware of the right of the first-born to ask for a double portion, immediately responds: *'Please let a double portion of your spirit be upon me.'* Elisha's persistent zeal wins the day and he returns having obtained that for which his soul longed. He refused to take *no* for an answer.

I heard it said a number of years ago that the church in the UK suffers from two main problems: mediocrity and passivity. Having lived and travelled in various countries over the past twenty years, I have come to accept the accuracy of this observation. In the case of mediocrity, is it because we are afraid of spending the Lord's money? I'm not sure. But we certainly seem to lack zeal and creativity – even in how we advertise and present our conferences and church activities. As to passivity, we all too easily take *no* for an answer.

During my recent visit to Argentina, I was with a group of men from England one lunchtime. While looking for a suitable place to eat we walked into a restaurant which was closed for business although the front door was open. The immediate response of the group was to exit the dining room.

'Hold on, everyone,' I called out, 'perhaps the owner might welcome eleven hungry Englishmen.'

Our interpreter explained to the proprietor that we would all like a meal. 'Si, si,' was his immediate response. Thirty minutes later we were all enjoying the most delicious steak any of us had ever eaten. I still feel a little guilty about being responsible for disturbing the siesta of a waiter who was having forty winks under one of the tables! However, we did leave him a nice tip.

## Steer clear of self-interest

Each member of the team should be devoid of self-interest. To include in the team anyone whose main interest is to find a place for his or her own ministry is unwise, no matter how gifted that person is. Otherwise you run the risk of seeing a spirit of competition invade the whole team.

One of the most delightful things we observed in the King of King's Church in Buenos Aires was the manner in which the four leaders who were spiritual sons to Claudio Freidzon served their father in the Lord. These men were pastors with considerable responsibility in the church, but all of them were perfectly content to work under Claudio's leadership and to make his life as stress-free as possible. It reminded us of Timothy's relationship with Paul – which contrasted with that of other leaders whose self-interest precluded a close working relationship. After Paul tells the Philippians that he is sending Timothy to them, hc says:

> *'For I have no one else of kindred spirit who will be genuinely concerned for your welfare. For they all seek after their own interests, not those of Jesus Christ. But you know of his proven worth that he served with me in the furtherance of the gospel like a child serving his father.'* (Philippians 2:21–22)

Referring again to the team that surrounds Billy Graham, can you imagine the havoc that one of them could cause if he wanted to shift the attention from Billy

Graham to himself? Imagine Cliff Barrows wanting the crusades to be called the *Billy Graham and Cliff Barrows Crusades*. The next thing we would expect is for George Beverly Shea to insist on calling them the *Billy Graham, Cliff Barrows and George Beverly Shea Crusades* (except that he might take issue with Cliff Barrows over who would get second billing). No, these godly men understand the principle of working *for the good of the whole*, and as a united team, they have been able by God's grace to impact the entire globe with the gospel.

## Make room for risk takers

God is not impressed with people who are unwilling to take risks. The man in the parable who buried his talent because he wanted to 'play it safe' incurred the wrath of his master, who ordered him to be cast into outer darkness where there was weeping and gnashing of teeth.[11]

Every member of the team needs to operate in the realm of faith and be a risk taker. People who are known to take risks may seem a little arrogant at times, and they are capable of making some awful *faux pas*, but they are the sort of people whose lives make a difference. Thomas Myerscough once said of the young W.F.B. Burton: 'He's a difficult young man, but he will go a long way.' And indeed he did!

When Billy Graham came to Harringay Arena to conduct his first major crusade in Britain many years ago, the odds were heavily stacked against him. The Press ridiculed his youthfulness and inexperience – not to mention his every word and action. But Billy's heart was full of faith, and he ended up taking London and the Home Counties by storm. His courage had the galvanising effect of releasing many young people to share unashamedly their faith in Christ. I was one who, through his example and inspiration, began to take every opportunity to testify fearlessly of Jesus. As a cadet in the Metropolitan Police at the time, I saw nine other cadets receive Christ into their lives.

## Don't include 'stupid' people on your team

Proverbs 12:1 tells us that *'he who hates reproof is stupid.'* That's a rather direct statement – but it is also a profound truth. You are asking for trouble if you include people on your team who are not able to take correction. Nothing is more wearying than when you take precious time to adjust the words or behaviour of someone on the team, and he responds by making excuses or rejects out of hand the concerns you have just expressed.

There are some people whom I prefer to correct by talking in generalities because, if I give them instances of what I have observed, they will turn around and pull my observations to pieces. (*Any* point can be argued if one is inclined that way; the law courts demonstrate that principle daily.) It is even worse correcting someone who has the dubious knack of turning the whole conversation around, so that you end up being the one receiving correction. When that happens, I usually back out of the discussion by saying, 'You know, you may be right.'

The first part of Proverbs 12:1 says, *'Whoever loves discipline loves knowledge,'* and in Proverbs 9:8 we read, *'Reprove a wise man and he will love you.'* People who are teachable are a joy to have around. However, some leaders insist on trying to bring correction to people who are clearly not interested. In those cases, Proverbs 9:7–8 applies:

> *'He who corrects a scoffer gets dishonour for himself ... Do not reprove a scoffer, lest he hate you ...'*

## Team members must be able to endure hardship

Jesus never promised us that serving him would be a 'bed of roses'. His own life included many times of hardship and suffering – as did the life of the apostle Paul, who, next to Jesus, had the greatest impact on the world. As we noted previously, Paul's list of hardships included: hunger, thirst, sleeplessness, exposure to the elements, imprisonments, beatings, shipwrecks, threats, betrayals, and even stoning (to the point of apparent death). He then turns to Timothy and invites him to suffer hardship with him *'as a good soldier of Jesus Christ.'* [12] Some invitation! It must have been quite a challenge to be a disciple of Paul.

Members of apostolic teams who cannot cope with a little hardship can be a serious drain on the morale of the rest of the team. During much of my life I have travelled to third world countries. During these 'adventures', I have experienced a variety of night-time discomforts: sleeping on the floor, sleeping three to a bed, being visited by rats and plagues of 'creepy-crawlies.' In fact, at this very moment of writing, my back is covered with numerous itchy spots, wounds acquired as a result of my recent battles with mosquitoes, bed bugs and fleas in East Africa.

At times I have felt so ill – because of something I ate or drank on one of these visits – that I have wanted to die. I am not saying there haven't been moments of self-pity but, when this happens, I force myself to contemplate that in a few days' or weeks' time I will be back home, sleeping in my own bed and enjoying all the comforts of western society. It's then that I think of all those who, for the sake of the gospel and their love for Christ, have left those comforts behind permanently.

So when I find a member of my team whining about the plane being late or the food not being to their liking or some other petty complaint, I take the opportunity to remind them of those who face *real* hardship – those who, because they are serving Jesus on the 'front lines', have to overcome inconveniences every day while dealing with various deprivations, loneliness, disturbed sleep, malaria and a host of other life-threatening experiences.

A little suffering for Jesus never did anyone any harm. If someone cannot cope with small inconveniences while serving Jesus in a country like England, how would he ever manage if God placed him in the jungles of Peru, or alongside Jackie Pullinger amongst the drug addicts within the old walled city of Hong Kong? Thousands of years ago the prophet asked a similar question:

> *'If you have run with the footmen and they have tired you out, then how can you compete with horses? If you fall down in a land of peace, how will you do in the thicket of the Jordan?'* (Jeremiah 12:5)

## Self-initiators are essential

There is a profound difference between someone who is *independent* and someone who can take initiative and act independently.

Some years ago I read a riveting non-fiction book entitled *The Enigma*. The setting of the story was the Second World War and the desperate attempts by the allied forces to capture the secrets of Germany's communication system for its U-boats and warships. The key to the system was a machine nicknamed the *Enigma*, which enciphered messages into an unbreakable code. The time came during the war that hand-picked men were to be parachuted behind enemy lines to try to capture the *Enigma* and smuggle it back to England. One of the qualities required in those to be selected was their ability to be creative and act on their own without needing to consult with London. They were described as 'maverick types'. I will always remember reading that phrase and hearing God whisper in my spirit, *And those are the sort of people you need to make room for and delegate responsibility to.*

Every member of your team should be a self-starter who has the confidence to get on with the job and not be afraid of you. Paul could leave Timothy on his own in Ephesus for three years. Even though Paul had to encourage Timothy to be more bold, he obviously trusted him to handle the job.

## The need for self-discipline

I once heard it said that the highest form of human government is self-control. In his letter to Timothy, Paul sets out the goal of self-discipline: *'Discipline yourself for the purpose of godliness.'* [13]

It makes life unnecessarily difficult for the team leader if he has to keep on reminding members of their specific responsibilities, or keep on addressing issues like tardiness. I used to be known as the 'late' Barney Coombs because of my reputation for arriving late. Somehow I always felt I had a valid explanation for these late arrivals – until someone pointed out to me that my tardiness dishonoured those who were kept waiting for my arrival, and therefore, this was a sin against my brothers and sisters. Now that got my attention – and led to a change in my conduct.

If team members have their own agenda or priorities which cause them to be continually late, you should consider seriously whether you can afford to keep them. One person's late arrival of five minutes, while ten people are waiting, amounts to fifty lost minutes. Thirty minutes late – now your team has wasted five working hours! It soon mounts up.

Team members should also demonstrate self-control and discretion in their speech. The apostle James tells us that those who are able to control their tongue are able to control their whole body as well.[14]

The most important area of self-discipline, however, is in prayer and Bible study. When each member is spending quality time in personal devotions, the team will already be tuned into the Lord and to each other when they come together for ministry. And when team members are on their own, they can be trusted to be drawing the necessary nourishment that will keep them spiritually healthy and alert.

## Integrity is essential

Each member of the team ought to have earned the trust of the other team members. Their words should always be truthful and reliable – no exaggerated accounts. On more than one occasion I have experienced the acute embarrassment of confronting a situation based on the report of a colleague – a report which I believed to be accurate, which turned out to be highly embellished.

I have discovered that people who are careful in how they report on little things are usually trustworthy when it comes to bigger matters. I take special note of people who correct themselves in mid-sentence, because it tells me the little bell in their conscience has just rung, and they are making an immediate response.

Don't allow suggestive talk, especially with the opposite sex. Paul told Timothy to treat younger women as sisters, *'with absolute purity.'*[15] And don't be totally trusting of someone who never admits to making a mistake or who never confesses to sinning.

## Humility versus haughtiness

Nothing brings more discredit upon an apostolic team than when members behave with a haughty spirit. In Proverbs 6:16–17, we find that haughtiness is the first in a list of six things that God hates. In the Psalms, David says:

> *'You save the humble*
> *but bring low those whose eyes are haughty.*
> *No one who has a haughty look*
> *and an arrogant heart will I endure.'*[16]

Recently I attended a large renewal conference in the UK. I had been invited to share a few words at one of the main sessions, so the young man I am going to refer to knew that I was a leader. At the end of the meeting, many people were being prayed for; some had fallen to the ground in response to the moving of the Holy Spirit, including a twelve-year-old boy. As I finished praying for one of those who had come forward, a young man in his mid-twenties, a member of a team from North America, rather pompously beckoned me over with his forefinger to where the young lad was lying on the floor.

'Do you see this?' he said. 'This is a sign that God has a plan for the young people of this country.'

I thanked him for his observation and thought to myself, *If this young man's team leader would have witnessed this scene, he would not have known where to hide his face.*

1 Peter 5:5 tells us that God is *opposed* to the proud. You don't need people on your team who are in the process of being opposed by God. In fact, their removal from the team could well be the way God chooses to deal with their pride. Each member, like their Lord and

Saviour, should display a humble spirit and be willing to do menial tasks. As Jesus exhorted us in John 13:14:

> *'If I then, the Lord and Teacher, washed your feet, you also ought to wash one another's feet.'*

However, one word of caution is necessary: just because a person moves out in faith and confidence doesn't necessarily mean that he or she is acting proudly. Sometimes those who suffer from unbelief and fear are offended by those who are risk-takers. We should not mistake godly courage for fleshly arrogance.

## The team as a model

Finally, the whole team should *model* the biblical characteristics of body life. We cannot expect a local church to live according to these principles if the team that teaches them does not model them as well. The following could be called the ten *Golden Rules* of body life:

1.   *They should be devoted to one another in brotherly love* (Romans 12:10).
2.   *Each one should regard the others as more important than himself* (Philippians 2:3).
3.   *They should give preference to one another* (Romans 12:10).
4.   *They should, through love, serve one another* (Galatians 5:13).
5.   *They should be joyous and carry a positive demeanour* (1 Thessalonians 5:6).
6.   *They should encourage and spur one another on* (Hebrews 10:24–25).
7.   *They should walk in forgiveness* (Colossians 3:13).
8.   *They should do all things without grumbling* (Philippians 2:14).

9.  *They should strive to maintain the unity of the Spirit* (2 Timothy 2:24).
10. *They should confess their faults to one another* (James 5:16).

## *Footnotes*

1   Matthew 23:9.
2   Ephesians 4:16 speaks of the body *'being fitted and held together by that which every **joint** supplies...'* The word *joint* here refers to *relationships*.
3   Matthew 12:30.
4   1 Corinthians 4:17.
5   Philippians 2:20.
6   1 Samuel 3:19.
7   Jeremiah 1:6–7.
8   2 Chronicles 24:1.
9   DIY is the common term for *do-it-yourself* in the UK.
10  John 2:17.
11  Matthew 25:14–30 *Talent* here is a sum of money, but the same principle applies to any resources given to us – including gifts and abilities.
12  2 Timothy 2:3.
13  1 Timothy 4:7.
14  James 3:2.
15  1 Timothy 5:1 *NIV*.
16  Psalm 18:27 *NIV*, and Psalm 101:5 *NASB*.

# Chapter 7

# The Nature of a True Spiritual Son

The concept of having a father or mother other than your birth parents is difficult for westerners to accept and understand. That is not the case in many other cultures. For instance, there is a well-respected African leader with whom I have walked for a good number of years who, when he writes to me, addresses me as *Daddy*, and signs off with *Your loving son*.

We have already spoken about the importance of fatherhood, but in the next two chapters I want to develop the theme of *spiritual fatherhood* and *spiritual sonship*, and deal with some of the practical dimensions of those relationships. To avoid sounding tedious, I may not repeat the prefix *spiritual* when I refer to fatherhood or sonship.

It is crucial that before we start talking about the practical aspects of fatherhood and sonship that we settle the issue of its biblical origin. We cannot afford to base our theology and practice just on someone's good ideas! To list just a few examples: Eli became a spiritual father to Samuel, calling him, *'My son'* (1 Samuel 3:6); Elijah spiritually adopted Elisha, who called him, *'My father, my father'* (2 Kings 2:12); Paul adopted Timothy, whom he addressed as *'my true child in the faith'* (1 Timothy 1:2) and *'my beloved and faithful child in the Lord'* (1 Corinthians 4:17); Paul refers to Titus as *'my true child in a common faith'* (Titus 1:4); and of Onesimus, Paul says, *'my child, whom I have begotten in my imprisonment'* (Philemon verse 10).

Although there are many teachers and preachers, the fact is there are not many fathers. During the course of my life I have been instructed and inspired by many wonderful men of God, but there have been only four men – besides my natural father – whom I could say were spiritual fathers to me. Paul says something very similar in his letter to the church at Corinth:

> *'For if you were to have countless tutors in Christ, yet you would not have many fathers; for in Christ Jesus I became your father through the gospel.'*

(1 Corinthians 4:15)

The nature of a true spiritual son is not something that can be taught in a classroom. It comes by revelation and unfolds over a period of time. Just because someone leads you to the point where you put your trust in Jesus Christ does not mean that that person is your spiritual father. If such were the case, there would be countless fathers – contrary to what we read in 1 Corinthians 4:15.

Evangelists are more like spiritual midwives: they *bring* to birth but they don't *give* birth. In fact, only the triune God gives birth – through the miracle of regeneration. But as the concept of *fatherhood* is used in the New Testament, it has to do with the ability to draw together a spiritual family and to raise them up in Christ. Thus, Paul's use of the term *through the gospel* is not limited to the experience of justification by grace through faith, but includes the good news of ongoing sanctification by grace through faith.

With this in mind, let me go on to suggest seven qualities that you can expect to see in a true spiritual son.

## 1. He has a kindred spirit with his father

Paul could say of Timothy, *'I have no one else of kindred spirit'* (Philippians 2:20). The word rendered *kindred* here could also be translated *like-minded*. It literally means *of equal soul*. A son who is walking submissively and with a *kindred* spirit will not always have to think through what needs to be done. It's already in his heart.

A leader once said to me, 'Barney, tell me what is expected of me, then I will know what I have to do.' I tried to explain to him that true family doesn't work like that. If it did, the result would be a 'performance' mentality: it would be the letter of the law, not the spirit. And nothing kills relational life faster than living by the letter of the law.

Of course, I'm not ruling out presenting goals and discussing how these goals should be achieved. That would be helpful communication. But in the case just cited, I was looking for a relationship that, over a period of time, would establish in his heart something of our *family genes*, while he was looking for the rules so that he could conform to them and then get on with his own agenda. He was thinking that by his obedience to the rules, he would earn a place in our spiritual family – rather than taking the time to cultivate relationships, watching what we did, and gradually discovering the rationale behind our *modus operandi*. Solomon said to his sons:

> *'The beginning of wisdom is: Acquire wisdom; and with all your acquiring, get understanding.'* [1]

## 2. He is thoroughly fulfilled in serving his father

A true son does not compete with his father because he

understands that he has part ownership in the 'family business'. Some years ago I was listening to a young man tell the story of how his grandfather had started *The Firs*, a well-known conference centre in Bellingham, Washington (in the north-western United States). I was fascinated to keep hearing this young man say 'we' when he was describing the challenges faced by his grandfather as they developed the retreat centre – especially because he had already told us he wasn't even born when it all got started around the turn of the century.

I was reminded of this *ownership* concept only last year when we took three-year-old Leighton, one of our grandsons, on our boat. At first he would refer to the boat as 'Grandad's boat', but after a few rides and the opportunity to sit on my lap and steer, he started saying, 'My boat'. In some strange way, he understood that he was included in the ownership of his grandad's boat. Belonging and ownership are somehow inseparably linked.[2]

I usually could tell when people were about to leave a church in which I was the leader. They would start using the word *you* instead of *we*, and *yours* instead of *ours*. They obviously no longer saw themselves as part of the family nor responsible for anything that occurred within it; their words betrayed their true feelings.

Let me repeat: a true son is fulfilled in serving his spiritual father. In 1 Kings chapter 19 we read of Elijah casting his cloak over the shoulders of Elisha while he was ploughing with the oxen, signifying that one day his prophetic mantle would rest on Elisha's shoulders. In verse 21 we read:

> *'So he returned from following him, and took the pair of oxen and sacrificed them and boiled their flesh with the implements of the oxen and gave it to the people*

and they ate. Then he arose and followed Elijah and
ministered to him.'

We find the same picture in Philippians 2:22 where Paul
says of Timothy:

> 'He served with me in the furtherance of the gospel like
> a child serving his father.'

## 3. A true son is a 'clinger', not just a 'kisser'

What do I mean by this strange statement? These
metaphors come from the story of Naomi and her two
daughters-in-law, Ruth and Orpah. Naomi's husband and
both sons had died, so she decides to return home to the
land of Judah.

After commencing her journey, Naomi stops and
explains to Ruth and Orpah that it would be far better
for them to return to their own people in Moab. All three
women start weeping loudly, but Ruth and Orpah refuse
to go. Once again, Naomi pleads with them to return and
again, all three start weeping loudly. Then the Scriptures
say this: *'And Orpah kissed her mother-in-law, but Ruth
clung to her.'* This is followed by a profound statement of
covenant on Ruth's part:

> '[F]or where you go, I will go, and where you lodge, I
> will lodge. Your people shall be my people, and your
> God, my God...'                                (Ruth 1:16)

A true son is not a 'fair-weather friend'. He is in the
family for the long haul; he is not just a starter, he is also
a finisher!

## 4. He is of proven worth

A true son is not a 'Johnny-come-lately'. There will be longevity in the relationship – not to mention loyalty and concern for his father's reputation. This, despite the fact that there are no perfect fathers – whether in the natural family or the spiritual.

Noah, for all his great accomplishments, was not a perfect father either. But when he lay exposed in his tent because of drunkenness, two of his sons chose to honour him: they covered his nakedness – for which they received a blessing that was passed on to succeeding generations. A true son will not expose his father's shame, for he sees himself included in the shame of his father's mistakes. Paul may not have made any major mistakes – other than his persecution of the church prior to his conversion – but if he had, it is unlikely that Timothy would have been disloyal. Paul says of him: *'But you know of his proven worth...'*[3]

## 5. He is content with being his father's faithful envoy

This principle was, of course, most perfectly exemplified in the person of Jesus:

> *'I do nothing on my own initiative, but I speak these things as the Father has taught me.'*          (John 8:28)

Paul writes of Timothy that *'he will remind you of my ways which are in Christ.'*[4] This is not an inferior role (as someone might suppose). I have watched some who have hankered after their own identity, their own work, only to find that when they finally got it, they didn't have the grace to see it succeed. So instead of being in the vanguard of something that was making a significant difference, they ended up in almost total obscurity. It's a sad sight. If only they had been content to stay in an envoy role and be part of a powerful, dynamic team, they could have had great influence.

Timothy seemed to be comfortable being Paul's assistant, yet was entrusted with major responsibilities on Paul's behalf – apostolic leadership in several strategic churches including Corinth, Ephesus and Philippi.

## 6. A true son will press in and draw life from his father

A true son doesn't need his father running after him to impart wisdom and counsel. On the contrary, he will run after his father (press in) because he is wise enough to realise that his father has accumulated a rich store of distilled wisdom over many years. Listen to what Solomon writes to his sons:

> *'Hear, O sons, the instruction of a father,*
> *And give attention that you may gain understanding,*
> *For I give you sound teaching;*
> *Do not abandon my instruction.*
> *When I was a son to my father,*
> *Tender and the only son in the sight of my mother,*
> *Then he taught me and said to me,*
> *"Let your heart hold fast my words;*
> *Keep my commandments and live;*
> *Acquire wisdom! Acquire understanding!*
> *Do not forget, nor turn away from the words of my mouth.*
> *Do not forsake her, and she will guard you;*
> *Love her, and she will watch over you.*
> *The beginning of wisdom is: Acquire wisdom;*

> *And with all your acquiring, get understanding.*
> *Prize her, and she will exalt you;*
> *She will honour you if you embrace her.*
> *She will place on your head a garland of grace;*
> *She will present you with a crown of beauty."*
> *Hear, my son, and accept my sayings,*
> *And the years of your life will be many.*
> *I have directed you in the way of wisdom;*
> *I have led you in upright paths.*
> *When you walk, your steps will not be impeded;*
> *And if you run, you will not stumble.*
> *Take hold of instruction; do not let go.*
> *Guard her, for she is your life.'*      (Proverbs 4:1–13)

Notice that last sentence. Basically it says: instruction is your life! When a son draws instruction from his father, he is, in effect, drawing life.

There are even times when words are unnecessary; just the presence of the father suffices. Thirty-one years ago, having left my job to serve the Lord as a pastor, I suddenly found myself under some unexpected financial pressure. Instinctively, I caught a train to Whitstable, Kent, to my parents' home and spent several hours just relaxing in my father's presence. We didn't discuss my problem because there was no need to tell him; it was enough just to sit with him and draw from his strength. I returned home that evening with a heavy weight having been lifted off my shoulders, knowing that everything was going to be all right.

## 7.  A true son adjusts how he follows, not how his father leads

An egalitarian person always knows best. He 'sells' his own ideas and wisdom (no need to buy when you have it all). He always knows a better way of doing it, whether his opinion is asked for or not. Ironically, the one person in history who *could* have rightfully done things his own way, the Lord Jesus, instead lived in perfect reliance upon his Father, and followed his lead – all the way to the cross.

> *'Truly, truly, I say to you, the Son can do nothing of himself, unless it is something he sees the Father doing; for whatever the Father does, these things the Son does in like manner.'*　　　　　　　　(John 5:19)

Jesus knew that following his Father's lead did not detract in any way from his identity, his manhood, his fulfilment, his success, and his ultimate glory. Would that we also had such revelation – primarily in relation to our heavenly Father, but also in the way (and to the degree) that this principle applies to our earthly fathers. In the next chapter we look in more detail at spiritual fatherhood.

### *Footnotes*

[1] Proverbs 4:7.
[2] This type of *ownership* has to do with family and belonging – which is very different from the *ownership* mentioned in Chapter 4 which referred to a possessive attitude.
[3] Philippians 2:22.
[4] 1 Corinthians 4:17.

# Chapter 8

## The Nature of a True Spiritual Father

A father has a clear revelation that God has called him to that role. As we have seen already, fathers are relatively few in number, and in an age where fatherhood has been all but lost, there is a desperate need for such men to be recognised and received.

For instance, there are many men pastoring churches today who themselves have never been fathered – either by their natural fathers or any spiritual fathers. Such men tend to be insecure, and for that reason are usually defensive when offered well-meaning advice or (in some cases) well-deserved criticism. When they are given input that could help increase their pastoral effectiveness, they interpret it as disapproval. They see correction as rejection and react emotionally, often ending up with feelings of self-pity.

The blessing and security that comes through fatherhood is essential for such men, and they might well agree. But recognising the need and agreeing on the answer does not, in itself, bring the provision. I cannot promise anyone reading this chapter and who genuinely desires to receive fathering that it is readily available. What I can say is: *'The righteous man shall live by faith.'* [1] In other words, if you mean business with God and put your hope in him, I believe God will hear your prayer, and in his good time will provide for you the fathering your heart desires.

Let us go on then to examine a number of qualities that characterise a true father.

## He sees sons as non-disposable assets

A good father is not utilitarian. He doesn't use people, he *invests* in them! It is tragic to meet so many people in the church of Jesus Christ who feel they have been used. Deep down, many people feel that they are appreciated and included by leadership only because of their gifting: that their acceptance is based on what they can do, and not on who they are. And when their usefulness is gone, then so is the relationship.

Bob Mumford compares this to someone drinking a can of Coke and then throwing away the can. But that is not how God treats us, nor how a true father treats a son. A father is interested in *giving good gifts*[2], he seeks to *impart wisdom*, and he wants to *invest himself in the life of his son*.

## A heart that truly cares

Each time I read Paul's two letters to Timothy, I am impressed with the deep bond that existed between these two men. If I have been inspired to read these letters over and over again, Timothy must have been even more so. I picture him finding a quiet place where he will be uninterrupted, and poring over the letters, devouring each word as though it were a delicious morsel. I see the tears flowing down the young man's face and onto the paper. If ever a son encountered the true love and care of a father, Timothy found it on those pages.

Not only that, he also experienced the special strength that comes from a father's unqualified approbation. Added to that, he heard the urgent tone in Paul's voice calling him to dig deep into his inner being to find the courage in Christ to take his place on the front lines – spreading the gospel and establishing strong churches throughout the Gentile world. Listen to his words:

> *'This command I entrust to you, Timothy my son, in accordance with the prophecies previously made concerning you, that by them you may fight the good fight.'* (1 Timothy 1:18)

He challenges him to discipline himself for the purpose of godliness (1 Timothy 4:7). You can almost hear the entreaty in Paul's voice as he appeals to his son:

> *'O Timothy, guard what has been entrusted to you...'* (1 Timothy 6:20)

He exhorts him to suffer hardship as a good soldier of Jesus Christ (2 Timothy 2:3); he warns him to flee from the love of money (1 Timothy 6:11); and to flee youthful lusts (2 Timothy 2:22).

He advises him as to how to address the older men and women: to do so respectfully as fathers and mothers; and to treat the younger men and women as brothers and sisters (1 Timothy 5:1–2). He counsels him to avoid quarrelling (2 Timothy 2:24); but at the same time to be on the alert for Alexander the coppersmith – he's dangerous (2 Timothy 4:14). Perhaps in part because of the load he was carrying, Timothy seems to have had a nervous stomach, and even this is included in Paul's care for his son:

*'Use a little wine for the sake of your stomach and your frequent ailments.'*

## Prayer on behalf of his sons

As was mentioned earlier, Paul prayed big prayers for the churches and the individuals under his care, often declaring that he prayed *night and day* for them. Whether the prayers are 'big' or 'little', a good father will be thoroughly consistent in praying for his sons. In this, we are also reminded of the example of Jesus, who as our High Priest – as well as our older Brother [3] and our Father [4] – intercedes for us continually.

## Mistakes can be stepping stones to success

A wise father allows his son to make mistakes. He is not a perfectionist when it comes to training his sons. He understands the proverb, *'Where there are no oxen, the stall is clean.'* [5]

I don't want to unsettle anyone who is about to have an appendectomy, but you can safely assume that the consultant [6] you have been seeing is not the one who will be operating on you. It will almost certainly be a doctor in training, and it may even be his first such operation. If so, he has previously practised only on cadavers, or assisted other doctors in the theatre. (A comforting thought, to be sure!)

A few years ago, as a result of picking up two bugs in Africa which caused cirrhosis of the liver, I was regularly attending the John Radcliffe Hospital, Oxford, for checkups. At each appointment, a blood sample was necessary. I vividly remember on one visit the consultant asking me if I minded a trainee doctor taking my blood. 'I need to tell you it will be her first effort,' he quietly added.

My mind went to the above-mentioned proverb – which also happens to be one of my favourite verses in the Bible. I recited it to the consultant, telling him it was necessary that I practised what I preached. I wish I could tell you that all went well, but that would be untrue. After several heroic attempts and a few words of encouragement from her boss, the trainee doctor finally managed to extract her phial of blood, but the bruise hung around for several weeks before it finally vanished.

In the book entitled *The Making of a Surgeon*, the story is told of a young surgeon performing his first append-ectomy under the watchful eye of the consultant. Nervously, the trainee took hold of the scalpel and tried to make an incision at the required spot. Suddenly the consultant slapped his hand and the scalpel fell to the floor. Beads of perspiration began to form on his brow as the nurse handed him another one. Again, his trembling hand took hold of the scalpel.

'Don't scratch him!' shouted his boss. 'Stick it in, man, stick it in!' Which is exactly what he did, except that he stuck the scalpel in too far, and what should have been a three-day recovery period for the patient ended up being three weeks.

Whether it is surgeons, bus drivers, airline pilots, or church leaders in training – all have to practise some-where. I will always be grateful for those who endured my early attempts at preaching. But it was too much for some members of the church. One lady, together with her daughter and son-in-law, wrote to me that they were leaving the church because my preaching was too shal-low. It was a long letter in which she cited a number of examples – all of which happened to be true. However, I still felt miffed with her attitude.

Several years later I found some of my old sermon notes and was quite taken aback with the shortage of content I found in them. I turned to my wife Janette and reminded her of the story and the letter of resignation, and then made this remark: 'do you know what, sweetheart, if I had to sit and listen to this stuff Sunday after Sunday, I think I would have resigned from the church as well.'

When a genuine father is observing his son's mistakes, he will be careful not to be too quick to make negative comments. He knows that by accentuating the positive, he will get more of the same, and will also build up a nice amount of 'credit' in the bank of approval that will help to cover the 'withdrawals' of correction that will be necessary at a later date.

In closing this chapter, I would offer a word of caution. As mentioned previously, Paul is a wonderful example to us in many respects. But just as we cannot expect all apostles to measure up to his apostolic level of faith and gifting, neither should we expect all spiritual fathers to be 'supermen' in the Kingdom of God. It may be true that the spiritual father whom God chooses for a man with major leadership and ministry responsibility is also a man with such responsibility, but we should remember that – whether in the natural or the spiritual – *fathering* usually has more to do with relationship, identity and character development than it does with ministry. Thus God may choose men whom the world considers quite ordinary to be extraordinary fathers. As Paul said to the Corinthians – who were so prone to the foolishness of prideful association (*I am of Paul, I am of Apollos, I am of Cephas*):

> 'Brothers, think of what you were when you were called. Not many of you were wise by human standards; not many were influential; not many were of noble birth. But God chose the foolish things of the world to shame the wise; God chose the weak things of

*the world to shame the strong. He chose the lowly things of this world and the despised things – and the things that are not – to nullify the things that are, so that no one may boast before him.'*

(1 Corinthians 1:26–29)

## Footnotes

1   Galatians 3:11.
2   Luke 11:11–13.
3   Hebrews 2:11, 17.
4   Isaiah 9:6 One of his names is *Everlasting Father*.
5   My translation of Proverbs 14:4, which rather graphically describes a basic principle of life and ministry: we can have everything neat and tidy, but only if no work is being done!
6   The term used in North America is *specialist*.

# Chapter 9

## Sons are Formed and Developed

In this chapter I want to suggest a number of ways in which a spiritual father draws out and develops a son. But in order to be able to share my heart fully, I need to present my thoughts as one who believes God has called him to be a father and who is received as such by a number of people. I trust the reader will be gracious and overlook any ways that appear to be self-promotional, as that is not my intent.

Before we address some of the specifics of this subject, I want to emphasise the point that having a *mentor* will always be more effective in someone's formation than just receiving *information*. This truth is finding wide acceptance by others – including executives in the business world as they seek the best forms of leadership and management training.

Mentoring can find its best expression in the church, where the quality of relationship and the significance of mission are at their highest potential level. Eugene Peterson puts it so aptly in his introduction to Paul's letter to the Philippians:

'This is Paul's happiest letter. And the happiness is infectious. Before we've read a dozen lines, we begin to feel the joy ourselves – the dance of words and the exclamations of delight have a way of getting inside us.

But happiness is not a word we can understand by looking it up in the dictionary. In fact, none of the qualities of the Christian life can be learned out of a book. Something more like apprenticeship is required, being around someone who out of years of devoted discipline shows us, by his or her entire behaviour, what it is. Moments of verbal instruction will certainly occur, but mostly an apprentice acquires skill by daily and intimate association with a 'master', picking up subtle but absolutely essential things, such as timing and rhythm and 'touch'.[1]

With this principle in mind, let's examine some of the ways that sons are formed and developed.

## The need for revelation

The starting point for a spiritual father is a revelation that this person has been entrusted to him to be raised as a son.

Twenty years ago my family and I emigrated to Canada where I joined the ministry team of a church in Vancouver, British Columbia. Shortly thereafter I was invited to the wedding of one of the couples in the church. It was during the reception that my attention was drawn repeatedly to the young man who was the master of ceremonies. The gracious manner in which he addressed everyone, the skilful way in which he moved the proceedings along – all pointed towards someone who clearly was cut out to be a leader.

I knew that he was already the co-leader of a house group in the church, and I was aware that he was to be in charge of the children's camp to be held in the summer, but apart from that, he was a stranger to me. During the buffet meal, I heard what I believe was the 'still, small voice' of the Lord saying, 'I am joining you to him.'

I wish I could say that at that precise moment, a bolt of lightning hit the ground, or the sun broke through the clouds, but no such thing occurred. There was just a quiet sense that God had spoken and that he would bring it to pass. Apart from the occasional greeting, there was no contact until I bumped into him at the children's camp and found myself asking him how he had come to join the church and what his plans were for the future.

'Well,' he said, 'I had finished my degree course at Edmonton University and had become aware that young people were being discipled at this church, so I decided to move to Vancouver because I wanted to become a man of God.' Then, with a note of disappointment in his voice, he added, 'But nobody picked me up.'

Without thinking, I blurted out, 'How about giving me a try?'

He thought for a moment, then shaking his head he replied, 'No, that's not possible. I've been accepted back in Edmonton to complete my Teacher Training Diploma as I hope to become a teacher.'

'But,' I persisted, 'isn't it possible to take that course in Vancouver?'

'Yes it is, but it's too late; the final date for registration has passed.'

I still felt an urging in my spirit not to take *no* for an answer. 'Listen,' I said, 'why don't you pray about it, and if the Lord gives you peace, why not approach the University of British Columbia and see if they have a vacancy?'

And that is how Ron MacLean ended up becoming my true son in the Lord.

## Spending time together

In Mark 3:14 we read:

> *'And he appointed twelve, that they might be with him, and that he might send them out to preach.'*

Before Jesus was willing to send the disciples out to preach, he wanted them to spend quality time with him. Before Timothy could be trusted to be left at Ephesus – to lead the church and to guard the saints from false teaching – he first of all had to spend valuable time being discipled in Paul's ways in Christ:

> *'And the things which you have heard from me in the presence of many witnesses, these entrust to faithful men, who will be able to teach others also.'*
>
> (2 Timothy 2:2)

As soon as Ron MacLean had finished his diploma course at the University of British Columbia, he, together with three others, accompanied me on a four-week visit to India and Nepal. For the past thirty-one years, it has been my practice to take others with me when I travel outside of my home church. In the last six weeks, I have taken ten leaders with me to Argentina and four Bible College students to Kenya and Uganda. At the moment of writing, I am sitting in a cottage in a small village just outside Zagreb, the capital city of Croatia. In the room next to me are two sons in the Lord; together we have been planning a major outreach scheduled to take place this summer in war-torn Bosnia.

I will always be grateful to my father who made it a practice to take me with him whenever he went out preaching. As early as ten years of age, I learned to be comfortable standing before people in a pulpit, reading the Scriptures, announcing a hymn and, later on, leading them in prayer.

To illustrate how seriously we view this principle in our family of churches, we received an offering of £25,000 last summer at our *Days of Destiny* camp, an offering whose sole purpose was to train young people with leadership potential, enabling some of them to accompany me on my international travels. There is no substitute for time spent together, sharing heart to heart.

There is a vast difference between passing on information and sharing the deep thoughts and feelings of one's heart. In John 15:15, Jesus says:

> *'No longer do I call you slaves; for the slave does not know what his master is doing; but I have called you friends, for all things that I have heard from my Father I have made known to you.'*

I have many precious memories of time spent with my father, especially when I accompanied him on his ministry trips. In spite of the fact that he was nearly fifty years old when I was born, we were still able to communicate well; his frequently shared stories from his youth and early years helped in bridging the age gap.

My father liked to predict advances that science would make in my lifetime. I remember him 'prophesying' that one day, football matches would be played at night under powerful spotlights. (I could hardly imagine such an amazing event.) I recall the time he said that one day, every family would have a radio in their home that would show *pictures*.

He also spoke to me about his special interests. For instance, he loved the people of Israel and often spoke of the suffering they had endured at the hands of the Nazis.

He spoke of the battles he had fought during the First World War, and some of the amazing escapes he had made. But there is one special moment I will never forget. One night we were walking along a country lane that cut through a wooded area. It was almost pitch black, but we were able to find our way in the dark because of the sound of a stream that ran along one side of the road.

But what seemed to be quite a pleasant sound – albeit a little eerie in the darkness was in fact bringing back some fearful memories to my dad. Suddenly he stopped and said, 'Do you hear that water?' Not waiting for an answer he continued: 'I can remember one night during the war hearing that same sound when we were holed up in some woods in France. We knew the Germans were just a few yards away, but there was nothing we could do. It was so dark we couldn't see a thing, neither could we hear anything because of a stream that was running nearby. Normally you could hear some movement – such as a twig breaking – but this night, all we could do was crouch there in the blackness, terrified for our lives, straining to pick up the slightest noise that would warn us of the enemy's advance. Every time I'm in the dark and hear the sound of running water, I feel that same fear returning.'

It was one of those special moments in a young boy's life that draws him very close to his dad. The huge gap that existed between a sixty-three year old authority figure and his son was dramatically reduced to almost zero, as I was allowed a rare opportunity to peer inside my father's soul and see my real dad with real fears. This unique moment of vulnerability helped me to understand what a man really feels when death is only a few feet away, staring him in the face.

Even the great apostle Paul felt the need to be vulnerable: to share some of his hurts and disappointments with

136

Timothy – for instance: *'At my first defence no one supported me, but all deserted me.'*[2] He also reminds Timothy of the fact that *'all who are in Asia turned away from me,'*[3] even mentioning two of the culprits by name.

## Giving assignments

Another way of developing sons is by giving them assignments that require self-discipline and study. The written assignments I have handed out ranged from 'Discover all the places where Christ is revealed or referred to in the Old Testament,' to 'Explain what you understand by *Restoration Theology*, using no more than two sides of a foolscap page.'

It doesn't take long to discover those who take such an assignment seriously, and those who treat it as something of a joke. Those who are self-indulgent and undisciplined always end up making a half-hearted effort, whereas those who are zealous and hard-working invariably produce more than you ask for. (I think the record is 35,000 words, and that person is currently serving Jesus in East Africa.)

## Praying together

There are a number of senior leaders in the UK who will always be indebted to the *Prayer and Bible weeks*, which were organised every New Year by Denis Clarke, Campbell McAlpine and Arthur Wallis. I learned more about prayer at those conferences – and in the presence of these men – than anywhere else.

It was the influence of these men on my leadership at Basingstoke Baptist Church in the late sixties and early seventies that led to our days of prayer and fasting, our nights and half-nights of prayer, and on one occasion – a whole week of prayer and fasting. Every Saturday night I would drive to a hill near Hatch Warren that overlooked Basingstoke, and pray over the town. Later on, together with others, I would lay hands on the pews and intercede for those who would be occupying them the next morning.

In 1976, a few months after we had moved to Vancouver, I again began to gather a few potential sons on Saturday nights for the purpose of prayer. And again, we would pray over every seat in the church building. Some nights I would walk into the hall to find them on their faces, pounding the floor with their fists, interceding for our church and for our city. Those were wonderful days.

## Imparting your life message

What is a life message and why is it so important? Most theologians would agree that Luke's life message dealt with the humanity of Jesus and was expressed through an accurate record of *'all that Jesus began to do and to teach,'*[4] and what Jesus continued to do by the Holy Spirit through the acts of his apostles.

John's life message was to prove that Jesus was the Christ, the Son of God, so that by believing, people *'might have life in his name.'*[5] John continues in the same vein in his epistles. In 1 John 4:2 he says,

> *'By this you know the Spirit of God: every spirit that confesses that Jesus Christ has come in the flesh is from God.'*

Later on, in verse 9 of the same chapter, he writes,

> *'By this the love of God was manifested in us, that God has sent his only begotten son into the world so that we might live through him.'*

In his second epistle, he warns the *'chosen lady and her children'* that there are many deceivers who have gone out into the world, who do not acknowledge that Jesus Christ has come in the flesh.[6]

On a personal level, my life message can be found in these two passages:

> *'[Y]et for us there is but one God, the Father, from whom are all things, and we exist for him; and one Lord, Jesus Christ by whom are all things, and we exist through him.'* (1 Corinthians 8:6)

> *'And he gave some as apostles, and some as prophets, and some as evangelists, and some as pastors and teachers, for the equipping of the saints for the work of service, to the building up of the body of Christ; until we all attain to the unity of the faith, and to the knowledge of the Son of God, to a mature man, to the measure of the stature which belongs to the fullness of Christ. As a result we are no longer to be children, tossed here and there by waves, and carried about by every wind of doctrine by the trickery of men, by craftiness in deceitful scheming; but speaking the truth in love, we are to grow up in all aspects into him who is the head, even Christ, from whom the whole body, being fitted and held together by that which every joint supplies, according to the proper working of each individual part, causes the growth of the body for the building up of itself in love.'* (Ephesians 4:11–16)

Everything I do that relates to the body of Christ and everything I preach and teach is motivated, structured, and impregnated by these two passages. This is my life message, and I take every opportunity to pass it on to my sons. It is also the purpose and motivation behind writing this book.

## Bringing correction

Hebrews 12:7 says,

> *'For what son is there whom his father does not discipline?'*

Recently I spoke a word of correction to a young pastor with whom I was travelling – a word which I knew would probably keep him awake that night. The next day, I couldn't help noticing the heaviness of soul that was revealed all over his countenance. He also seemed to be keeping his distance from me. However, later that day I could sense his spirits lifting so I went over to him, put my arm around him and asked him how he was doing. 'I'm recovering,' he responded with a painful smile.

I followed up my question by asking, 'Why should *I* be the only one who received correction from a father in the faith – with the result of sleepless nights?' We laughed together, and I told him of an occasion at Capel Bible Week in 1974 when Bryn Jones and I had come to the conclusion that a well-known preacher who was visiting from another country was indwelt by an unclean spirit. Later, Bryn unwisely shared our conviction with Arthur Wallis, who was one of the speakers. That evening, Arthur took each of us aside and told us in no uncertain terms how wrong and dangerous it was for us to judge another brother without any evidence.

I had a terrible night. I think it was about 3:00 am when I finally dropped off into a fitful sleep. The next morning I eyed Bryn as he approached me – looking like he had been dragged through a hedge backwards, big bags under his eyes, his usual upbeat spirits noticeable by their absence. 'So how did you sleep last night?' I enquired.

He looked furtively about him as if someone were spying, on him and then asked, 'Did Arthur talk to you yesterday evening? Cor, I didn't half get a roasting! The sun was up before I finally got off to sleep.'

We were blessed young men to have a father who loved us enough to correct us.

## Dealing with character flaws

In my book *A Guide to Practical Pastoring*,[7] I talk about the 'doughnut hole' principle. I refer to a quote from a wall plaque that I saw in a pastor's study. It said, *What a man builds because of his giftedness can be destroyed in a moment because of his character*. Isn't that the truth! That is why it is so important to make sure your sons have the character qualifications to be entrusted with ministry 'inheritance'.

It was this issue that Solomon spoke of in one of his bleak commentaries in Ecclesiastes:

> *'Thus I hated all the fruit of my labour for which I had laboured under the sun, for I must leave it to the man who will come after me. And who knows whether he will be a wise man or a fool? Yet he will have control over all the fruit of my labour for which I have laboured by acting wisely under the sun.'*
>
> (Ecclesiastes 2:18–19)

Paul tells the elders at Ephesus to be on guard for themselves and for all the flock (Acts 20:28). In this particular case, Paul is referring to the possibility that after he has gone, false teachers – or as he calls them, *savage wolves* – will come in, not sparing the flock. All his hard work over a period of three years (*admonishing each one with tears*) would have ended up being wasted. He also feels concern for Timothy – as we noted earlier – warning him to flee from such snares as lust and the love of money.

## Drawing out the gift

God has placed a particular deposit of grace in each believer. There is no one better than a spiritual father to recognise that gift and to draw it out. It's sad that in far too many cases, pastors view gifted people in their congregation as assets to be exploited rather than gifts to be developed. When this happens, any persons whose gifts become more visible than the pastor's soon find out that they are perceived as a threat instead of a blessing, and so their services are squeezed out.

For someone's gift to be drawn out requires a father's precious time and attention. Let me illustrate. A young man whom I believe will go a long way in ministry and who already leads a congregation agreed, at my suggestion, to send me two cassette tapes of his messages so that I could evaluate his preaching. As a result of this exercise, he is now being far more careful in his interpretation (for example, in using words such as *legalism*), and he is attending speech therapy classes.

Practice makes perfect! Unless opportunity is given for people to practise preaching or leading a meeting, how will they ever grow and develop? A perfect meeting is not always the best meeting. Bob Mumford talks about the difference between a 'perfect meeting' and a 'perfecting meeting'. When we make sure our gatherings include opportunities for our up-and-coming leaders to participate, we are preparing for the future. In the long run, aiming at perfect meetings yields a poor return. True success is producing successors!

## Imparting blessings

*'Now Joshua the son of Nun was filled with the spirit of wisdom, for Moses had laid his hands on him . . . '*
(Deuteronomy 34:9)

*'And for this reason I remind you to kindle afresh the gift of God which is in you through the laying on of my hands.'*
(2 Timothy 1:6)

While I was writing this book I discovered that one of my fathers in the faith, Sid Cheale,[8] was terminally ill with cancer and was not expected to live more than a few days. As it happened, I was within a hundred miles of Shrewsbury where he lived and was able to see him before he died. Sid's face lit up with joy as I popped my head around the corner of his bedroom door. As I leaned over to give him a kiss, he grabbed my hand and immediately began to prophesy over me. I could feel the goose bumps rising. It was like Ephraim and Manasseh receiving Israel's blessing, or Jacob receiving the birthright blessing from Isaac. It was a powerful, unforgettable moment.

After I sat down, Sid told me that without telling anyone else, he had asked the Lord if he could be allowed to live long enough to see Michael Pusey and myself. He said, 'Last week Michael came to see me, this week you have come; now I'm ready for Father to take me home.'

Together with Michael Pusey and Derek Reynolds, I had the privilege of speaking at his funeral service. When I stood up to address the congregation, I introduced the three of us as 'Sid's boys' – and so we were.

Whether in life or at the time of death, a father seeks to impart blessings to his sons. And what a treasure that blessing is!

## Establishing sound doctrine

A spiritual father cares about his son's doctrine being sound. That was certainly true in the case of men like Arthur Wallis and Willie Burton; more than once I found my doctrine being questioned and adjusted by these men of God.

I remember sitting at the same meal table as Mr Burton while discussing a certain matter from Scripture with the person sitting opposite me. Even though the great man was at the other end of the table, he still managed to pick out my conversation – to which he added his own comment: 'Brother, don't read into the Scriptures what isn't there.'

Paul was extremely interested in Timothy's doctrine, exhorting him:

> *'Be diligent to present yourself approved to God as a workman who does not need to be ashamed, handling accurately the word of truth.'* [9]

Some people play down the need for sound doctrine, claiming that love is the only thing that counts. But they fail to understand that truth is one of the basic dimensions of God's character; it cannot be 'downgraded' to a secondary level or 'separated' from the others:

> *'Lovingkindness and truth have met together;*
> *Righteousness and peace have kissed each other.'*
> (Psalm 85:10)

> *'Jesus said to him, "I am the way and the truth and the life . . . "'* (John 14:6)

> *'And we beheld his glory, glory as of the only begotten from the Father, full of grace and truth.'* (John 1:14)

## Providing training

A father encourages his son to pursue the proper training and equipping that will enable him to reach his full potential in Christ. I'm sorry to say that at this point in time, many leaders in the 'new churches' are ill-equipped to lead and carry the governmental responsibilities that they now find thrust upon their shoulders. They had set out on what seemed like a Sunday afternoon charismatic ramble in Kathmandu valley, but now, with no base camp to support them, they find themselves struggling up Mount Everest, ill-prepared and ill-equipped.

In our family of churches we have recognised the urgent need to address this problem, and as a result, have invested considerable time and money into the training of young leaders. With Bible schools in Scotland, Canada, New Zealand, India (and one soon to open in Uganda), we are seeking to put things right.

Having said that, I want to emphasise that theological training is certainly not the only way of preparing people for God's call on their lives. Whether we are called to medical work, economics, education, computer programming, construction trades – whatever it is – it is all God's business and requires from us the finest training and preparation in order to be the most influential and effective people possible. The objective of this training is not being 'successful' in worldly terms, but rather fulfilling our mandate to be God's *salt and light* [10] in this world.

## Recommending further resources

By recommending books, tapes, conferences and seminars, a father helps to enlarge his son's spiritual understanding of God's word and ways. He does not regard his own resources as sufficient to meet all of his son's needs: for his son to fully mature in his calling in God, he will need the input of others.

A wise father is not possessive. He understands the dangers of what farmers call *inbreeding*. When the same bull is used to impregnate three or more generations of cows in the same family, the first cow produces a normal calf, the calf's offspring will be weak, *its* offspring will be born deformed, and the last generation will die shortly after birth. I would not go so far as to draw an exact parallel with the dynamics of spiritual fatherhood, but I would say that both the Scriptures and the example of the early church would teach us the importance of receiving input from the various other members of the body of Christ.[11]

Every year it is my practice to give as Christmas presents books that will challenge and stimulate the thinking of those who receive them. In 1994 I gave out a book by David Wells entitled *No Place for Truth*. This last Christmas I gave out John Piper's excellent book *The Pleasures of God*. (In fact, I bought another seventy-five copies of it for our European Leaders' Conference in January.)[12]

Similarly, I have felt that it was important to bring into our own leader's conferences other ministries from other 'streams' of the great river of God – men who will bring us something that we may lack, or open our eyes to things that we do not see as clearly as we should. We may not agree with every small detail of doctrine and we may do things quite differently in our church family, but the value of this kind of 'cross-pollination' can be considerable.

## Encouraging full disclosure

Fathers, never allow your sons to hide their cards close to their chest. Train them to take risks and walk in the light.

If a son never tells you what he really thinks, how can you challenge his thinking? If he is having a problem with the way you are handling him, but never discloses the fact, how will you know whether you need to adjust your ways? On the other hand, it may be that *he* has an attitude problem.

It always grieves me deeply when I discover that a close colleague has had a problem with me for a considerable time and has not shared it with me. That kind of scenario suggests he may have a problem with self-preservation, or *I* may have a problem with not being sufficiently approachable. Either way, it does not speak well of the level of trust and freedom that a close relationship in the body of Christ should exemplify.

A son who has learned to 'play it safe' will never grow up to take risks in God. Indecisive and tentative leadership causes more frustration in the body of Christ than anything else I know. One of the greatest gifts you can give your son is to teach him to walk in full disclosure (especially in terms of close relationships), to be decisive, and to take risks in God. Good decision-makers make good problem-solvers.

## Instilling discretion and prudence

Discretion and prudence are vital characteristics of a good leader. In Proverbs 8:12, Solomon wrote to his sons (and to anyone else willing to listen):

> *'I, wisdom, dwell with prudence, and I find knowledge and discretion.'*

Someone who is unable to keep a confidence ends up being distrusted, and someone who cannot be trusted soon loses the credibility to lead.

A discreet person has learned how to control his tongue. He is not given to exaggeration, nor does he try to impress others by how much he knows (or thinks he knows). Proverbs 17:28 makes an excellent observation:

> *'Even a fool, when he keeps silent is considered wise; when he closes his lips, he is counted prudent.'*

Now that puts discretion and prudence within everyone's reach!

Prudence involves acting with, or showing, care and foresight. Here is a simple yet practical example of its application. The father of one of our leaders had died, so I rearranged my schedule in order to attend his funeral. I thought it would be an opportunity for Tim, a son in training, to travel with me. The problem was that he wasn't properly dressed for the occasion, and when I suggested that he needed to go home and change into more formal clothing and put on different shoes – instead of the jogging shoes he was wearing – he started to react.

'What's wrong with my jogging shoes?' he protested.

'Everything is wrong with them,' I insisted. 'They are not appropriate, they will dishonour the family and they will dishonour us.'

Well, being a good disciple, Tim did as he was told and returned appropriately attired. We managed to find seats at the back of the chapel with the intention of slipping out and returning to the church office as soon as the service ended. However, unbeknown to us, it was decided that at the end of the service all the guests, starting from the back, were to come forward and file past the coffin in full view of the family of the deceased who were seated in the front row.

When we finally got outside, Tim let out a big sigh and exclaimed, 'Brother, am I ever glad that I listened to you.

I don't know where I would have hidden my face if I had turned up in my jogging shoes.'

## Allowing life's struggles to be God's training ground

A person watching a butterfly trying to escape from its pupal shell has to resist the urge to help. Entomologists tell us that if we help a butterfly out of its chrysalis, it will be unable to fly; in fact, our act of 'kindness' will consign the poor thing to an early grave. The very act of struggling is the means by which the winged creature is equipped to fly. As it twists and turns in its heroic effort to extricate itself, blood begins to be pumped into the wings; once out, the wings expand and usually within an hour the little creature is airborne.

The hatching of a gosling provides another picture of the value – in fact the absolute necessity – of struggle in the formation of healthy life. In the process of hatching, the gosling's determined gyrations and repeated pecks at the shell not only allows it to break out, it also forces the yolk up into its stomach. This provides food for the first few days, without which the gosling would survive only a few hours.

There is an important lesson in these parables from nature. A wise father refuses to make life too easy for his sons, because such an act of 'kindness' may interfere with the essential growth and development process designed by God. That principle is true in both the natural and the spiritual family. Have you noticed that children who are spoiled by their parents are, more often than not, ill-prepared for adult life? One of the reasons is that they have never learned to handle disappointments or any form of deprivation. They expect to get their own way and to be waited on by others – rather than following in the footsteps of Jesus who *'did not come to be served, but to serve.'*[13]

I believe that one of the mistakes made by many of the newer churches[14] was that leaders who left their secular employment to take up full-time leadership of a church were usually paid a salary equal to that which they received in their previous job. The intention may have been good – providing for the needs of their family, giving *honour* to the leading elder (in the 1 Timothy 5:17 sense) – but the effect may have been to rob the new leader of an opportunity to exercise faith, thus cutting short an important step in his development.

I'm now grateful for the financial struggle that Janette and I experienced when I resigned from the Metropolitan Police and we moved to a cottage in Cliddesden, a small village, one and a half miles outside of Basingstoke. It was a two-bedroom cottage with no hot water, no sewerage, and no bathroom. The outside brick shed contained a chemical toilet that required emptying once a week. The kitchen – if you can call it such – was large enough for only one person to work in.

Within a few weeks of our arrival, I went north to attend Capernwray Bible School, leaving Janette behind to manage the house and take care of our two young children, all on the princely sum of five pounds a week. When we had first arrived from London, my thoughts were that I would start house groups in the villages surrounding Basingstoke, and somehow God would provide for our needs. Whether this was presumption or faith I'm still not quite sure, but I can testify that God wonderfully provided for us in ways that we never could have imagined.

By the time I returned from Bible School, Michael Pusey had resigned from Basingstoke Baptist Church and had moved to take the pastorate of Farnborough Baptist Church. This, of course, left a vacancy at Basingstoke. By now, our meagre savings were exhausted – apart from six shillings and eight pence remaining in our bank account.

Within a few days, Stan Barnden, the church secretary, contacted me and asked if I would be willing to take care of the church on seven pounds a week until they got a pastor. The following week I took up my new respons-ibilities. Arthur Harvey, the church treasurer, decided to pay me in advance, and on my first Sunday in charge, handed me an envelope containing twenty-eight pounds. Only God knows why he made that decision.

But seven pounds a week was not enough; we needed ten pounds, ten shillings. Within a short time, John and Viv Bellegulle, a delightful, vibrant couple in the church, came to see us. John had been invalided out of the Airforce and received a weekly disability pension of three pounds ten shillings. The Bellegulles were full of smiles and excitement as they said to us, 'God has told us that we are to start giving this money to you.' We could barely hide our relief. God was taking care of our needs in a big way!

A few months later, however, John came to me with a serious look on his face: 'Barney, I'm afraid God has told us that we are to stop giving you the pension money.' I cannot remember my exact response, but I do know that there was no panic in our household, for we were begin-ning to learn that we had a heavenly Father who, if we sought first his kingdom and his righteousness, would take care of all our needs.

The next day, Arthur Harvey came to me: 'Barney,' he said, 'the deacons have decided to increase your stipend to ten pounds ten shillings a week.'

I first met Ted Kent in 1969 through an advert in the *Redemption Tidings*. Ted was a car dealer in Gosport who had a heart for evangelism. Later that year, we agreed to visit Eastern Europe for the purpose of smuggling Bibles into Czechoslovakia, Hungary, Rumania and Yugoslavia. But before we could start the journey, we needed to get tickets for the cross-channel ferry and obtain our visas from the embassies in London. The day of our trip to London, Ted drove up from Gosport and met me at Alton Hospital, where later that day I planned to visit Janet Allen, one of our young people who was recovering from back surgery.

On our arrival in London, it was decided that Ted would go to the embassies while I would go to the travel office to purchase the tickets. Somehow I had got the idea that Ted, with a business of his own, would pay the fares for the ferry, but God had other ideas. While queuing up at the travel agency, the Lord spoke quite firmly and distinctly to me: 'I am not pleased with your understanding of where the finances are going to come from. You are relying on Ted Kent to be your provider and not me.'

It was a salutary lesson!

Right then and there I settled the issue that all the costs of this journey would be evenly split between us. So as soon as Ted and I met again, I made it clear that I expected to be fully responsible for my share of the expenses. With the visas acquired and the ferry paid for, we returned to Alton where I bade farewell to Ted and entered the hospital to make my pastoral visit. Just as I entered Janet's ward, Ann Robson, a ward sister [15] who was on duty in the adjoining ward, saw me and called out, 'Barney, would you drop by my office on your way out? I need to see you.'

'Sure, I'd be happy to,' I replied, wondering what it might be about.

Later in her office, Ann handed me an envelope. 'This is a little gift from Martin and me to help towards your expenses for Eastern Europe.' Then she added, 'You will notice that the amount has been altered. We had made the cheque out this morning, but whilst Martin and I were having our lunch, we both felt a strong impression that the Lord wanted us to double the amount.'

'What time were you taking your lunch?' I enquired.

'It was twelve-thirty,' she replied.

'That's amazing,' I told her. 'That was the precise time God told me I was to pay my share of the ferry fare!'

I opened the envelope and – yes, you can guess – the extra amount matched exactly my half of the fare. There is no substitute for experiencing first-hand the miraculous provision of God.

Without battles, we will never prove that God is a victorious warrior. Without sorrow, we will never know that our God is the God of all comfort. Without financial need, we will never experience for ourselves that our God is *Jehovah Jireh*, the Lord our provider. These incredible experiences laid a foundation of trust in the Lord that remains with us to this very day.

## Footnotes

[1] *The Message*, p. 485.
[2] 2 Timothy 4:16.
[3] 2 Timothy 1:15.
[4] Acts 1:1.
[5] John 20:31.
[6] 2 John verse 7.
[7] Barney Coombs, *A Guide to Practical Pastoring* (Eastbourne: Kingsway Publications, 1993).
[8] Coombs, *op. cit.*, pp. 72–73.
[9] 2 Timothy 2:15.
[10] Matthew 5:13–16.
[11] *'The eye cannot say to the hand, "I have no need of you"...'* (1 Corinthians 12:21). *'I planted, Apollos watered...'* (1 Corinthians 3:6).

12  I found John Piper's latest book *Future Grace* to be equally worth-while.

13  Matthew 20:28.

14  For example, those in the *House Church* movement in the UK and the *Discipleship* movement in the USA.

15  Comparable to a *head nurse* in North American hospitals.

# Chapter 10

## Can Women be Apostles?

One of the most basic tenets of evangelical teaching is the authority of Scripture: that the Bible is our only rule of faith and practice, the final 'Court of Appeal' for all questions of doctrine – great or small. As an Evangelical Christian, my response to the question *Can women be apostles?* must be found in Scripture, and not in personal preference.

Over thirty years ago I vowed that I always would adjust my theology and practice to biblical teaching whatever the personal cost – even if the cost was to lose the approval of my friends. I mention this because it is quite possible that some, after reading this chapter, will conclude that I am a male chauvinist. I am also aware that some of my friends who are apostolic team leaders have changed their views on the subject in recent years, and now ordain women to be elders and, in some cases, to be apostles. I wish them well, but I cannot help believing that they are making a serious mistake.

The issues raised by this question are not limited to women apostles; they apply as well to women elders. The roles of apostles and elders are both governmental in nature and are strongly linked to the biblical concept of fatherhood – which will be addressed at a later point in this chapter.

Because the disposition of spiritual government in the Bible clearly is male, the proponents of women apostles and women elders have had to try to find ways of explaining that disposition away. In this regard, the following arguments have been advanced:

1. That the Greek word *Kephale* in 1 Corinthians 11 means *source*, not *head*: that it involves the sense of *derivation* rather than *authority*.

2. That Jesus did not include women among the twelve apostles because the sphere of their ministry was limited to Israel and the presence of women in leadership would have been culturally unacceptable. Also that the same cultural issue arises in 1 Corinthians 14:34–35 and 1 Timothy 2:11–15 where Paul instructs the women at Corinth and Ephesus to remain quiet when the church gathers together.

3. That the patriarchy of the Old Testament is greatly reduced in the New Testament.

4. That through the cross, all differences between men and women relating to authority were cancelled.

5. That Paul proved he was in favour of women apostles by his use of feminine terminology.

6. That perhaps certain passages – 1 Corinthians 11 and 14 and 1 Timothy 2 – were added to Scripture by copyists.

7. That it is faulty logic to conclude that Jesus' choice of twelve men as apostles is relevant in terms of gender.

8. That Deborah's role as a judge and prophetess provides a biblical example of a female governmental leader.

9. That the apostle Junias (listed in Romans 16:7) was actually a woman.

Most of these arguments raise serious questions that deserve a thoughtful, biblical answer. In the remainder of the chapter, I shall try to provide such a response.

## 1. *Kephale*: Head or Source?

In Greek, the everyday meaning of the word *kephale* is purely and simply *head*. It is used of anything whose contribution has a sense of priority over others – whether it be the 'head' of a river or the 'heads' (that is, leaders) of clans in the Old Testament. The most scholarly handling of this Greek word that I have seen is by Wayne Grudem in *Recovering Biblical Manhood and Womanhood* in which he devotes 43 pages to the subject, leaving me with no doubt that the word *head* is in fact the most accurate translation of *kephale*.

The translation of *kephale* to mean *source* rather than *head* is thus highly questionable. But even if it were accurate, we still would be left with a unique place of authority being designated for men. If we translate 1 Corinthians 11:3 to read: 'The *source* of Christ is God,' we are still left with the fact of God exercising his authority in sending his Son – who did only those things that pleased his Father and who did nothing on his own initiative, and whose words and works originated with his Father. Are we therefore suggesting that this is the way a wife should submit to her husband who is the *kephale* in that relationship? It sounds no different from *head* in terms of authority; if anything, it seems to carry greater government.

It would seem that the more we examine *'kephale'*, the stronger is the biblical case for headship – both in terms of the word itself (the translation) and its broader meaning in the context of Scripture (regardless of which translation of the word is used).

157

## 2. Exegesis, culture, and the role of women

There is no question of the legitimacy of considering cultural and social conditions when exegeting Scripture. But this background information never should be taken to contradict the plain meaning of the text, nor seen to negate the general tenor of Scripture. That approach ultimately puts man's wisdom ahead of God's revealed truth – which, of course, is what liberal denominations have been doing for many years and with predictable results: scepticism concerning the miracles, endorsement of homosexuality, and so forth.

Much of the doctrinal teaching in the early church came in response to problems such as heresies, disorder, conflict and corruption.[1] The problems were serious, but their apostolic response gave us passages like 1 Corinthians 13 on love, Galatians 2:20 on being crucified with Christ, and 1 Corinthians 15:35–57 on the resurrection of the dead. We take all of this teaching to be *'inspired by God and profitable for teaching,'*[2] but wherever the apostle's response refers to God's order *before the fall*, we should take special note, because it has to do with God's ultimate intention, his original plan – and not a secondary plan or a concession (*'because of your hardness of heart'*[3]).

With that in mind, it is important to realise that when Paul teaches the church in Corinth on the subject of male headship (1 Corinthians 11), and instructs Timothy concerning women's behaviour in the gathered church (1 Timothy 2:9–15), that he does not address the issue from current cultural conditions, but from the example of Adam and Eve *before* they fell into sin. Here are some excerpts from the Genesis account to which Paul refers:

*'Then the Lord God formed man of dust from the*

*ground, and breathed into his nostrils the breath of life;
and man became a living being.'*　　　(Genesis 2:7)

*'Then the Lord God said, "It is not good for the man to
be alone; I will make him a helper suitable for* [4] *him."'*
　　　　　　　　　　　　　　　　　(Genesis 2:18)

We then read of God forming the animals and bringing
them to Adam who named them (a governmental act),
but none of them was suitable for (or *corresponding* to)
Adam. So God put him into a deep sleep and removed
one of his ribs, fashioning it into a woman. When Adam
awoke and saw her, he said (no doubt with a gleam of
approval in his eye):

*'This is now bone of my bones,
And flesh of my flesh;
She shall be called Woman,
Because she was taken out of Man.'* [5]

My old Pastor used to say of the Old and New Testa-
ments, *The New is in the Old concealed; the Old is in the
New revealed.* Thus it is that Paul, by the Holy Spirit's
anointing, helps to reveal the meaning of Genesis chapter
2. In 1 Corinthians 11:1–6 he first speaks of the headship
of man, then goes on to say in verse 7 that man *is the
image and glory of God; but the woman is the glory of man.*
This statement clearly takes us back to the Garden of
Eden: it is pre-fall and has nothing to do with Corinthian
culture. He continues:

*'For man does not originate from woman, but woman
from man; for indeed man was not created for the
woman's sake, but woman for the man's sake.'*
　　　　　　　　　　　　　　　(1 Corinthians 11:8–9)

Again, we need to remind ourselves that this was how God *intended* it to be from the beginning: it precedes the arrival of sin and the curse. (It may still sit uncomfortably with present-day sensibilities, and I will try to explain *why* in section four.) Paul then points out that in the Lord, *'neither is woman independent of man, nor is man independent of woman,'* because even though woman's origin was from man, his birth is through woman, and in any case, all things originate from God.[6]

Paul uses the same scriptural foundation in his letter to Timothy:

> *'But I do not allow a woman to teach or to exercise authority over a man, but to remain quiet. For it was Adam who was first created and then Eve.'*
>
> (1 Timothy 2:12–13)

This had no more to do with Ephesian culture (or the women's possible lack of education) than the previous verses had to do with Corinthian culture; this was simply a re-statement of the *pre-fall* pattern that God established. As I understand it, Paul is not allowing any public ministry by women that is *governmental* in nature. It was previously established that public praying and prophesying by women is acceptable.[7]

In 1 Corinthians 14 we have Paul addressing the problem of church members in local assemblies using the gifts of the Spirit in an undisciplined manner. There was excessive speaking in tongues without interpretation, too many prophecies in a single meeting, and the prophecies were not being properly weighed. In verse 29, he says: *'And let two or three prophets speak and let the others pass judgement.'* In verse 32, he adds: *'And the spirits of the prophets are subject to the prophets.'* Some take this verse to mean that the prophets were to exercise *self*-control in their exercise of their gift, but in the context of verse 29, I believe it has to do with being subject to the evaluation of other prophets. Then Paul adds verse 34:

> *'Let the women keep silent in the churches; for they are not permitted to speak, but let them subject themselves, just as the Law also says.'*

Paul has already made it clear in Chapter 11 that women can prophesy and pray in the meetings. So what sort of silence is he asking for? Various explanations have been put forward: that the women in Corinth were too noisy, or that Paul was simply responding to cultural pressures. But Paul does not give any indication else-where of trying to please people with his instructions – least of all the Corinthians! The context of this verse is the judging of prophecy, and *that* I believe is the key to understanding it. Women were not allowed to judge prophecy as this would subject male prophets to the government of women, thus breaking a pre-fall principle.

If my understanding is correct, then the overriding issue in these passages is *government*. In Ephesus, apparently, women were teaching doctrine in a way that was seen to be exercising authority over men; and in Corinth, women were overstepping the boundary by judging prophecy (quite possibly because men were failing to do so). Thus the apostolic correctives, which explicitly invoke the original (sin-free) pattern of God's creation.

## 3. Is patriarchy for today?

In some ways this is the most serious amongst the issues raised by the proponents of women apostles and women elders. By that I do not mean that this is their strongest argument, but that it has the most serious implications. It is not surprising that the secular feminist movement has targeted patriarchy as its main enemy: biblical patriarchy and the original Edenic order represent the two main pillars of male government – insofar as the home and the church are concerned. But an attack on patriarchy not only seeks to destroy one of these pillars, it also challenges the structure of the nuclear family and even the Trinity itself. That is obviously not the intention of anyone who loves the Lord, but that is potentially the effect.

God is a father. One of his names is *God the Father*. He is called the *Father of our Lord Jesus Christ* (2 Corinthians 1:3), and *God our Father* (1 Corinthians 1:2). Jesus not only taught us to begin our prayers with *Our Father*, he also shared an intimate portrait of his relationship with the Father and how that relationship is meant to include *us* (John chapter 17).

The fatherhood of God is eternal. He was God the Father before ever the earth was created and he will continue to be the Father throughout all eternity. Fatherhood is what distinguishes him from the other members of the Trinity in the same way that Sonship marks out Jesus from the Father and the Holy Spirit.[8] Without fatherhood we do not have true family. As Paul writes:

*'For this reason, I bow my knees before the Father (Greek – Pater), from whom every family (Greek – Patria) in heaven and on earth derives its name . . .'*
(Ephesians 3:14–15)

Elizabeth Elliot wrote:

'The feminist theology of Christians (I cannot call it "Christian feminist theology") is a Procrustean bed on which doctrine and the plain facts of human nature and history, not to mention the Bible itself, are arbitrarily stretched or chopped off to fit. Why, I ask, does feminist theology start with the answers? One who spoke on "A Biblical Approach to Feminism" defined her task (a formidable one, I should say!) as the attempt to interpret the Bible in a fashion favourable to the cause of equality (Virginia Ramey Mollenkott at the Evangelical Women's Caucas, Washington, DC, November 1975). The "interpretation" called for amounts to a thorough revision of the doctrines of creation, man, Trinity, and the inspiration of Scripture, and a reconstruction of religious history, with the intent of purging each of these of what is called a patriarchal conspiracy against women. Why must feminists substitute for the glorious hierarchical vision of blessedness a ramshackle and incoherent ideal that flattens all human beings to a single level – a faceless, colourless, sexless wasteland where rule and submission are regarded as a curse, where the roles of men and women are treated like machine parts that are interchangeable, replaceable, and adjustable, and where fulfilment is a matter of pure politics, things like equality and rights?"[9]

I believe it is impossible to attack patriarchy without involving the Trinity: fatherhood is just that basic. Since we were created in God's image, *his* fatherhood will of necessity be reflected in our human fatherhood – whether in the natural or the spiritual sense. It cannot be otherwise. That is one reason why I suspect Satan is behind the scene in this attack. The other reason is that Satan will always try to tear down what God builds up, and *family* is a prime example. If he can whittle back the strength of fatherhood, he can deal a devastating blow to the family. To picture it in naval terms, it's like firing a torpedo below the water line into the hull of the ship called *Family*, and it's only a matter of time before the ship sinks.

But God will have the last word. It was at another dark moment in history when Malachi prophetically ended the Old Testament canon with these words:

> *'And he will restore the hearts of the fathers to their children, and hearts of the children to their fathers...'*
> (Malachi 4:6)

## 4. Were women emancipated at the cross?

Yes they were – and so were men – but only from that which was part of the curse. Even then, not everything that came upon mankind because of the curse has been removed: women still have pain in childbirth and men still perspire when weeding their gardens. Some things will be restored only when Jesus returns. As the Scriptures tell us, the whole creation groans as it anxiously awaits its liberation.[10]

Redemptively we are all equal in the sight of God – we are *fellow heirs of the grace of life*[11] – but we are not *functionally* equal. This truth is so simple, yet so profound, that many people do not understand it. Perhaps that is because it is a singularly *counter-cultural* idea for those of us living in the Western world.

While the theme of *equality* has been with us a long time, we have seen a paradigm shift[12] in the last twenty to thirty years – and it all has to do with our definition of equality. I mentioned earlier in this chapter that we may be uncomfortable with a verse like 1 Corinthians 11:9 which states: *'for indeed man was not created for the woman's sake, but woman for the man's sake.'* Why do we find that so jarring to our western democratic sensibilities?

I would submit that it all relates to our understanding of the word *equal*.

When Canada adopted its new Constitution in 1982, it acquired a new *Charter of Rights and Freedoms*, the centrepiece of which was a section on *Equality Rights*. In the background documents that were issued by the government at the time, it was clear that *equality* was going to mean much more than just being equal before the law or having equal opportunity. There was a philo-sophical commitment to the notion of *equality of function*. In other words, the policy-makers had decided that for women – or any other identifiable group – to be truly equal meant to *function* the same as everyone else. If that meant putting women in the army, so be it. If it involved allowing the mentally-ill to vote, so be it. Equality now meant equality of function, and this view had the force of the Constitution behind it.

Consider now what the Bible teaches us about equality:

> *'Have this attitude in yourselves which was also in Christ Jesus, who, although he existed in the form of God, did not regard equality with God a thing to be grasped...'*          (Philippians 2:5–6)

Orthodox Christian doctrine through the centuries has affirmed both the divinity of Christ and the equality of the three Persons of the Trinity: the Father, the Son, and the Holy Spirit. But this equality has always been under-stood in terms of *essence*, *glory*, *intrinsic value* and *eternal existence*. That is why Philippians 2:6 can speak of Jesus being equal with Father God.

But this equality clearly does not rule out differences of *order* and *function*. Jesus, while being equal with the Father, is eternally the Son who delights to do the will of his Father; while the Holy Spirit eternally proceeds from the Father and the Son, again in a subordinate *functional* role. That leaves us with a choice: whose definition of equality do we accept? After which pattern shall we model our lives?

For 'Bible-believing Christians' the answer should be straightforward. We were created in the image of God: it is unthinkable to consider any other model. Yet we do so. Why? Because we are influenced by the cultural 'ocean' in which we swim. We may not have consciously embraced a secular, humanistic notion of equality, but those concepts and attitudes are all around us, and we imbibe them without realising it. Thus when we read about woman being created for man, we may wince inwardly, feeling that that represents blatant inequality or even denigration of women. In reality, all it speaks to is the creation *order* and *function* of men and women; it does nothing to detract from their equality of essence and being.

It does come down to an issue of faith: will we believe that the biblical pattern applies in our society – sophistic-ated and humanistic as it is? Or will we cave-in to the world's way of thinking? If Jesus is equal with God and submits to his will, can we accept that wives are equal with their husbands even if they recognise male headship? Although *hierarchy* is a negative term to many people, can we accept that the kingdom of God is still hier-archical in *function* simply because hierarchy is in the Godhead and it existed on Planet Earth even before Adam and Eve sinned? If so, we are walking in the admonition of Romans 12:2:

> *'And do not be conformed to this world, but be trans-formed by the renewing of your mind, that you may prove what the will of God is, that which is good and acceptable and perfect.'*

## 5. Did Paul's use of feminine terminology prove his support for women apostles?

For example, in 1 Thessalonians 2:7:

*'But we proved to be gentle among you, as a nursing mother cares for her own children.'*

I cannot conceive why this would be a problem (pun intended). Because I eat like a horse, doesn't mean I am in danger of thinking that horses are human. Paul is simply using a metaphor in the same way we all do – 'He drove like a maniac'; 'She flew like a bird' – we do it all the time.

## 6. Did copyists add to the Scriptures?

It is widely accepted that our text of the New Testament is just about as accurate as you can get.[13] The good news is that we have such a magnificent supply of manuscripts that there is almost no difficulty in determining the correct reading of almost any verse.

No doubt the ancient copyists did their part in improving grammatical presentation (especially if language usage had changed over the years). But if we believe that God has failed to preserve the original meaning of the text, we have no reliable authority with which to stand and preach before God's people (other than the 'authority' of our own opinions). The suggestion that copyists added to the New Testament Scriptures is ludicrous and any bona fide Evangelical would have nothing to do with such mischievous meddling.

## 7. The 'faulty logic' argument

This argument states that if women cannot be apostles because of their exclusion from the 'twelve', surely Africans cannot be apostles either, for there were no Africans among the 'twelve' – thus we are dealing with a case of faulty logic.

Well, this *is* a case of faulty logic, but for other reasons. One might as well add Englishmen and Chinese to the issue being raised. The point is: Africans, Englishmen and Chinese were not residing in Israel in those days, but women *were*. Approximately half the population was female. If Jesus didn't mind offending the Pharisees by touching lepers, eating with Zaccheus, and allowing a prostitute to kiss his feet repeatedly, you can be sure he would not have worried one iota about what they would think about his appointing a woman apostle. The fact that he did not do so does not 'prove' the case against women apostles; it simply is one piece of biblical evidence.

## 8. Deborah, the Judge and Prophetess

Does Deborah's rule as Israel's Judge provide a positive biblical example of a woman exercising government over men? Well, despite the good she did, there are other facts to consider.

First of all, Scripture records in Judges 4:1 that Israel was once again doing evil in the sight of the Lord following the successful 80–year reign of Ehud. In verse 4, we have this telling statement:

> *'Now Deborah, a prophetess, the wife of Lappidoth, was judging Israel at that time.'*

Obviously the people of Israel were not following her

leadership. It wasn't until she summoned Barak and gave him a prophetic word which effectively made him Israel's military commander that Israel's fortunes changed. It seemed clear that Barak needed Deborah as a prophetess, and she needed him to lead the army governmentally.

One other verse that is relevant to the subject speaks of God's judgement against Jerusalem and Judah for their rebellious sins:

> *'Woe to the wicked! It will go badly with him, for what he deserves will be done to him. O my people! Their oppressors are children, and women rule over them.'*
>
> (Isaiah 2:11–12)

Why did God allow Deborah to rule over Israel? Most likely it was a judgement on the nation because of their sin. Otherwise, if someone insists on this case being normative, the same criteria would have to be applied to Samson, another 'exception' in that unusual period of the Judges.


## 9. Junias the apostle

There is some controversy concerning Junias, with some translations (e.g. King James) recording the name as Junia, which can be used as the feminine form – suggesting that this may be an example of a woman apostle. Because this raises a legitimate question of biblical interpretation, I will take some time to address it. However for a more thorough treatment, I would recommend the research of Wayne Grudem and John Piper in their excellent book *Recovering Biblical Manhood and Womanhood* (Crossway Books).

In answer to the question, *Was Junias a woman?* Grudem and Piper say the evidence is inconclusive.

However, in an exhaustive computer search of early Greek writings (ca. the ninth century BC to the fifth century AD) encompassing 2,889 authors and 8,203 works, they found only three cases of *Iounia*. The first was Plutarch (ca. AD 50–120) who makes this comment in *The Life of Marcus Brutus*: 'Cassius having married Junia, the sister of Brutus.' The second is Epiphanius (AD 315–403) who wrote an *Index of Disciples* which includes the entry: 'Iounias, of whom Paul makes mention, became Bishop of Apameia of Syria' (*Index Disciplulorum*, 125.1920). In Greek, the phrase *of whom* is a masculine relative pronoun (*hou*) and shows that Epiphanius considered Iounias to be a man. The third was John Chrysostom (AD 347–407) who made this comment concerning Junias: 'Oh! how great is the devotion of this woman, that she should be even counted worthy of the appellation of apostle!'

So there we have it. One church father says this person is a man, the other disagrees and says this apostle is a woman. Is the evidence for these positions equal? Grudem and Piper suggest that Epiphanius' comments are more conclusive because he seems to be more knowledgeable about Junias – recalling that Junias became Bishop of Apameia. They go on to add:

'Perhaps more significant than either of these, however, is a Latin quotation from Origen (died AD 252) in the earliest extant commentary on Romans: He says that Paul refers to "Andronicus and Junias and Herodian, all of whom he calls relatives and fellow captives (*Andronicus, et Junias, et Herodion, quos omnes et cognatos suos, et concaptivos appellat*)" (Origen's *Commentary on Romans*, preserved in a Latin translation by Rufinus, ca. 345– ca. 410 AD, in J.P. Migne, *Patrologia Graeca*, vol. 14, col. 1289). The name Junias here is a Latin masculine singular nominative, implying – if this ancient translation is reliable – that Origen (who was one of the ancient world's most proficient scholars) thought Junias was a man. Coupled with the quotation from Epiphanius, this quotation makes the weight of ancient evidence support this view.'

I realise that this subject can get very technical, but when doctrine is being established, we must be willing to do our 'homework': to subject our theories to the rigours of research and critical evaluation so that we develop a solid theological position. Without wishing to be uncharitable, I must admit I have been surprised by the dearth of substantive biblical evidence supporting the doctrine of ordaining women as apostles and elders. Its proponents bring to mind the strategy of a courtroom lawyer when he doesn't have a lot of facts to go on: by the use of a suggestion here, a question mark there, a snip of circumstantial evidence tossed underneath, and a liberal sprinkling of innuendoes thrown on top, he hopes to sow enough doubt in the minds of the jury to secure a victory for his client!

It reminds me of a little story involving our daughter Rachel when she was five years old. We were sitting having our evening meal when she suddenly asked, 'Daddy, how much does five noughts added to three noughts make?' [14]

'Nothing, sweetheart,' I replied, somewhat amused by her question.

'But Daddy,' she pleaded, 'They must add up to something – there's five of them and three of them.'

By now, the bemused looks had spread across the faces of the rest of the family. 'It still doesn't mean anything,' I said, trying desperately not to burst out laughing. 'If there were five million of them added to three million of them, the answer would still be a big nought.'

I certainly would not question the sincerity or integrity of those who ordain women to governmental leadership. Some are close, personal friends whom I greatly love and admire. Because of their outstanding godliness and because of our friendship, I have sometimes wished I could see their position in the Scriptures, but the more I search, the more I remain convinced that women apostles and women elders are not to be found in the Bible.

However, while we do not find them functioning as apostles in the Bible, we do see women as part of apostolic *teams*. Phoebe, a deaconess of the church at Cenchrea, probably carried the responsibility of delivering Paul's letter to the church in Rome. Paul commends her to the Romans and says:

> *'I ask you to receive her in the Lord in a way worthy of the saints and to give her any help she may need from you, for she has been a great help to many people, including me.'* (Romans 16:2)

Phoebe was clearly a part of Paul's team – as were Euodia and Syntyche who shared Paul's struggle in the gospel (Philippians 4:3). There is no question that women were involved in 'high-level' ministry in New Testament times, but that involvement did not include senior governmental roles in which they would be exercising authority over men. (Did that make them less important than men? Only if we believe that Jesus is less important than the Father because of his differing function and role.)

The Bible doesn't have an equal number of stories about women as men, but if we have eyes to see, there is ample scriptural evidence to confirm the intrinsic value and strategic importance of godly women – for example: Ruth and Esther, both of whom had Old Testament books named after them; Deborah and Huldah, recognised as prophetesses at a national level; Elizabeth, the mother of John the Baptist, Mary, the mother of Jesus; the women who accompanied Jesus on his travels throughout the cities and villages of Israel; Mary Magdalene and Mary the mother of James, who were the first to see the risen Lord and to be witnesses of his resurrection to the apostles; Joanna (wife of Chuza, Herod's steward) and Susanna, who were among those who helped support Jesus and his disciples out of their own financial means; Timothy's mother Eunice and grandmother Lois, whose godliness and faith were faithfully instilled in young Timothy.

The list is no less distinguished in this century. Consider the many thousands of godly women who sacrificed the comforts of home and the loving security of family – all for the sake of spreading the gospel of Christ in foreign lands: Gladys Aylward, Amy Carmichael, Elizabeth Elliot, to name a few. (By some estimates, twice as many women as men went out as missionaries.)

These are heroes of the faith whose lives are well-known to many, but I want to conclude the chapter by mentioning three women who have worked alongside me in the cause of Christ – and whom I also regard as heroes. *Annie Crowe* relocated to Uganda from England at my request several years ago and is now in charge of a number of Christian schools throughout the nation. While her excellent work and testimony has brought her in contact with high-ranking officials (including the President's wife, Janet Museveni), she also has endured the hardships of life in central Africa, including repeated burglaries of her home and the terrifying experience of being held at gun point by robbers who commandeered her car.

*Dr Jan White* pioneered medical clinics in Uganda as well as Kenya. Jan is one of the bravest people I know, whose exploits include crossing through no-man's-land during the civil war in northern Uganda. Jan is not only an excellent medical doctor, she is also a prophetess and a powerful preacher of the gospel through whom many have come to Christ.

*Karen Morgan*, who also moved to Uganda at my personal request, managed to set up a fully-functioning medical laboratory in the heart of the infamous Luweero triangle. By begging, borrowing and buying the necessary equipment and supplies, she has helped the medical staff at Kiwoko District Hospital save hundreds of lives – including many children.

These are three of the outstanding women who have served as part of my apostolic teams and who regard me as a spiritual father. I want to honour them for their outstanding faith, courage, and hard work in the gospel. Their role is not one which carries the *overall government* of the church (apostle, elder), but they function in a place of consultative leadership and vitally-important ministry. I would commend them as examples to the body of Christ.

### Footnotes

1  The list sounds disturbingly contemporary.

2  1 Timothy 3:16.

3  The reason Jesus gave in Mark 10:5 for the Mosaic law allowing divorce.

4  Or *corresponding* to him.

5  Genesis 2:23 In Hebrew, man is *Ish* and woman is *Ishshah*.

6  1 Corinthians 11:11–12.

7  Paul's reference in the next verse to Eve's (and not Adam's) deception suggests two things: that by responding to Satan's temptation, Eve

was acting independently; and that Adam's sin was deliberate: he was not deceived in the same way – making his sin all the more treasonous in nature.

[8] There is a sense in which Jesus is a father to us (as also are human fathers); thus there is one reference to him as *Eternal Father* in the list of names in Isaiah 9:6.

[9] *Recovering Biblical Manhood & Womanhood* (Crossway Books).

[10] Romans 8:19–22.

[11] 1 Peter 3:7.

[12] This may be a favourite term of New Agers, but it correctly describes the change in society's philosophical framework.

[13] See *Are the New Testament Documents Reliable?* by F.F. Bruce for further reading in this regard.

[14] In North America, *noughts* are called *zeros*.

# Chapter 11

## Apostolic Reviews

In the early 1970s[1] Peter Lyne, a long-standing friend, came to Basingstoke Baptist Church for a weekend of ministry. Until that time, we had been an autonomous (self-ruling) church. We had many visiting speakers – including such famous names as George Otis, founder of High Adventure Ministries and author of numerous books; and Pat Robertson, founder of the Christian Broadcasting Network. Nonetheless as a church, we had no place of organisational accountability other than an extremely weak connection to the Baptist Union (whose leadership neither understood nor approved of our charismatic beliefs and practices).

During the Sunday evening service, Peter suddenly broke off his message and addressed the congregation prophetically: 'The Lord says that you are to be an *Antioch Church* that will send out people to the nations.' It was an electrifying moment; you could have heard a pin drop.

The following week when I began to take a close look at the Bible references to the church at Antioch, I was struck by the fact that they not only sent out apostles, they also received governmental input from outside. That input began with the arrival of Barnabas, sent to them from Jerusalem, and later Paul, who was brought into the church by Barnabas. I noted that they received a governmental decision made by the Council of Apostles and Elders at Jerusalem, and that they received the decision by means of a letter carried by two Jerusalem prophets, Judas and Silas – even though Barnabas and Paul were returning to Antioch themselves at the same time. All this revealed that they were clearly not an insular, independent, self-ruling assembly. Its leaders were *not* tenaciously hanging on to power: they were interacting relationally and governmentally with the larger body of Christ. So where did this put us? I wasn't sure, but I began to make that question an urgent matter of prayer.

Up to this time, almost every new step we took – praying for the sick, exercising the gifts of the Holy Spirit, 'body ministry', 'team ministry', the introduction of elders, the abandonment of the Baptist form of democratic government – had all originated from personal direction that I believed had been received from the Lord. But with this prophetic word from Peter, I knew that from now on, things were going to be markedly different. And so it was that in the course of a growing relationship with Arthur Wallis, I began to view him not only as a personal pastor into my life, but also as an apostle to our congregation.

In the months that followed, we increasingly opened the door for Arthur to address governmental issues with the elders. At one point, when a dispute between one of the elders and myself had reached an impasse, we chose – by mutual consent – to invite Arthur, together with Campbell McAlpine, to arbitrate. As a result, peace was restored.

Although we were beginning to appreciate the blessing of receiving apostolic input, we still didn't think we had opened ourselves up in a vulnerable way to the man we called our apostle. We still found ways of holding onto the reins and protecting our precious autonomy. In 1974 I finally saw the damaging and inhibiting effect that resulted from the controlling spirit with which I was governing the church. I went to the elders and proposed that we invite Arthur, together with Bryn Jones, to come for a ten-day period (over two weekends) and examine every area of our church life – including both my leader-ship and my family. There were to be no restrictions on whom they spoke to and what they addressed (although when they interviewed other ministers in the town, I nervously wondered whether we had offered them too wide a warrant).

We all waited for Monday morning to come for the final list of recommendations to be delivered. It would be untrue to say there were no surprises. In fact, some of their observations were painfully shocking, but soon proved to be accurate. If my memory serves me correctly, apart from one item of their list, all the areas of concern were agreed upon and the problems rectified: the Basing-stoke Baptist Church 'wineskin' had just experienced a major renewal.

Since that time the church (now known as Basingstoke Community Church) has undergone three more reviews, including a recent one which resulted in the senior leader and his wife, David and Chris Richards, being released to a wider sphere of apostolic responsibility, with their place in Basingstoke being filled by David and Hazel Marchment who have been with the church for over twenty-five years. (This will be covered in more detail in the following chapter.)

In the remainder of this chapter I would like to offer some guidance to those involved in apostolic reviews – at both the giving and receiving end of the evaluations. (Some may think this is an example of where it is more blessed to give than to receive, but I'm not quite so sure. It can be quite an arduous experience for *all* concerned!)

## 1. Relational and covenantal links are essential

In the business world, it is quite common for firms to hire consultants to carry out an investigation (often called an *operational review*) into how the company is faring, and to make appropriate recommendations. However, there is a world of difference between a business and a church family. I believe it is crucial that whoever leads a church review team is someone who has a relational bond with the leadership of that church. First of all, it helps safeguard the people in the church from being handled in a careless, insensitive and cavalier manner. (Even then, I have found it necessary to apologise for not being caring enough in review situations.)

Secondly, that relationship safeguards the review team in the way that the final report is handled by the elders. Church reviews can have the effect of pulling the pin on a whole stack of 'hand grenades' that have been waiting for years to explode. Sometimes it is necessary to name names in order to speak honestly and thoroughly about a certain problem. In one review that I won't forget, I included the name of a man who was renowned for his history of church-hopping and who had been at the centre of controversy in each previous congregation. Even though I had requested that our report be handled in the strictest confidence and kept within the eldership, I discovered to my dismay that copies had been handed out to the entire church membership.

This review was the only occasion in which I did not have a relational bond with the leadership, and therefore was not received as having any apostolic authority. I was left in an extremely vulnerable position and vowed I would never again allow myself to be trapped in like manner.

## 2. Including the fivefold ministries

These days when we are invited to carry out an apostolic review, we consider it essential to include in the team someone representing each of the fivefold gifts,[2] someone with a heart for children and young people, and (especially if the church is fairly large) a woman who is able to evaluate the ministry to women. This enables the church under review to be examined in every department of church life by people who have expertise in these areas.

## 3. Confidentiality

One of the first things I ascertain when considering a request to lead an apostolic review is whether the leaders are willing for the church members to answer our questions and make comments in complete confidentiality. Unless we can guarantee that what is said will be held in strict confidence, people will be reluctant to participate, and without their participation, the whole exercise is futile. Of course, this arrangement requires a great deal of trust from those in leadership – a point which I always emphasise in the final report.

At the beginning of the review week – and with the permission of the elders – we announce a special dispensation for all who want to express a concern or tell us about what is bothering them. At the end of the week, we announce that the dispensation is over, and anyone who continues to murmur or complain is disobeying the Scriptures.[3]

## 4. Collecting data

We employ three ways of collecting data for the reviews, the first being *interviews*. We like to meet with all the elders *minus* the senior leader, then with the elders' wives, then with the next layer of leadership – house group leaders, youth leaders, worship leaders, and so on. After that, we like to meet with all those who would like to speak with us privately.

The second method is *questionnaires* (a sample copy of which is found at the end of the book). Again, people's anonymity is guaranteed. Along with the questionnaires, people have the opportunity to express their views in a letter.

Thirdly, we like to have an open meeting for all those who would prefer to share their opinions in a public forum. This may sound rather risky (some fearing the possibility of all sorts of acrimonious attacks on the leaders) but, in reality, it often gives us the opportunity to pull the sting out of hurting people and prevent much worse damage. However, the team members must keep in mind that their mandate is not to overreach the elders' authority and try to rectify the problems, but rather to listen, observe, and report their findings to the elders. We always take the opportunity to honour the leaders publicly, reminding the congregation that apostolic reviews are very rare in the body of Christ, and that they are a blessed people to have leaders who love them enough to make such a meeting possible.

## 5. Apostolic reviews are to inform the elders

During the week of the review, I normally spend a few minutes each day with the senior leader so that any serious complaints against him won't come as a major shock at the end. It also gives him an opportunity to question the accuracy of the complaints. After the week is over and the report is completed, we first schedule a private meeting with the senior leader to share our findings and recommendations with him personally. This is followed by a full presentation to the rest of the elders.

One of the mistakes I have made in past reviews is not being sensitive enough concerning those of whom the report is unfavourable. I believe that each person who receives 'low marks' ought to be treated with the utmost dignity by being allowed to hear our concerns personally and privately before the report is heard by the full eldership.

I must emphasise the need for sensitivity – especially at the conclusion of the review. After putting in seventeen- and eighteen-hour days all week long, and dealing with lots of intense feelings and situations, team members likely will feel exhausted. At such times, we need to draw on God's grace to be sensitive and gracious to all concerned – right to the end of the review week.

One of the things we make clear to the congregation is that the purpose of our review is to help inform the elders of problem areas, and to alert them to any dangers that may be creeping up unawares on them and the church. The report is not for general distribution to the congregation. What is later released to them will be what the elders deem appropriate. In recent years, we have also offered the elders the opportunity of inviting us back within six months to 'review the review' and to monitor the reality and effectiveness of changes they have sought to make.

In the next chapter, we go on to present some testimonies from senior leaders of churches which have benefited from apostolic reviews.

## *Footnotes*

1 As I recall, it was either 1972 or 1973.
2 Ephesians 4:11.
3 Legitimate concerns may be expressed any time, of course, so long as the proper channels are used.

# Chapter 12

## Testimonies

There are three testimonies in this chapter. The first is from Ron MacLean, who leads Gateway Community Church in Winnipeg, Manitoba, Canada. The second is from David Richards, who until recently led the Basingstoke Community Churches. David has now been released to lead apostolic teams. The third testimony is from Fraser Hardy, who leads the Christian Community Church in Palmerston North, New Zealand.

There is a saying that 'the proof of the pudding is in the eating.' It is my hope that these testimonies will demonstrate how the principles outlined in this book have worked out in real life situations – in three different church settings and on three different continents. This is 'the proof of the pudding.'

### A testimony by Ron MacLean

I was on the edge ... burnt-out. Worst of all, I didn't know it! My wife calls it 'momentum'. I was like a spiritual freight train hurtling down the track unaware that the bridge had been washed out.

The church had tripled in attendance in three years from

150 to 500 people, and the workload and corresponding pressures had multiplied with it. My spiritual well was dry, my relationships were strained and my leadership had an 'edge' to it. It was an ideal time for the saints (especially my wife and family) to have a church review. The apostolic team spent several days with every strata of church life – listening, asking questions, evaluating the leadership and hearing what the Spirit was saying to the church. Finally, the time came to share the comments, concerns and recommendations with the elders.

I was nervous and feeling a bit defensive. As it turned out, with good reason. The team's first concern was about me. 'We are concerned for the pastor,' they said. 'He is stressed out and doesn't know it!'

That's when it happened. With lightning reflexes I jumped up and indignantly objected, 'I am not!' (What an unjust accusation!)

Everyone laughed. I had been ambushed; blinded by my own momentum. The penny dropped. I started to laugh and meekly took my seat again, amazed that the spiritual freight train had come so close to hurtling over the washed-out bridge.

The apostolic team's first recommendation was that our family take an extra two weeks for our forthcoming summer holiday. It was the longest vacation we had taken in our twelve years of service with the church. With every week came an increased appreciation of just how stressed out I had been. My wife, in particular, became a greater champion of apostolic input.

The church's first contact with apostolic ministry had been in 1976, three years before I arrived. It had been a cry for help. The original pastor's marriage was in trouble. Within weeks of the call for help, his wife ran off with the associate pastor. The church was devastated. The leadership was not formally accountable anywhere and the people began to scatter. In desperation they called across the nation to the only ministry with whom they had any contact. A relationship of love and trust was born out of that very difficult time. From that initial contact an apostolic team began working with a group of thirty-five very precious but very bruised people.

Over the ensuing few years the church was sent pastoral and teaching ministry every two weeks. Eventually an interim pastor was sent for ten months and finally God provided a permanent pastor, all through the love, faithfulness and perseverance of the apostolic ministry. At the invitation of those who were working apostolically with the church, my wife and I became God's answer to the prayer for that permanent pastor.

For over sixteen years we have had the privilege of receiving the wisdom, insight and objectivity of apostolic ministry. We have had two full church reviews and several mini-reviews. More than once we have been saved from disastrous decisions and painful oversights. Out of the pastoral and prophetic insight of apostolic ministry, the church has been spared the ruin of a 'split' on at least one occasion. Apostolic ministry has also provided our leaders and the church with a place of appeal. The congregation knows that if the elders are not listening to them, they have our encouragement to contact those whom we receive apostolically. This has brought a tremendous sense of peace, security and protection to all of us.

Apostolic ministry has facilitated vision where there have been blind spots; building where there has been just gathering; and change where we have settled for the status quo. We have been exposed to a wider perspective than the local church and have had the privilege of fellowship with the body of Christ in other nations.

Paul wrote to the Corinthians,

*'For though you might have ten thousand instructors in Christ, yet you do not have many fathers.'*

(1 Corinthians 4:15a)

We have had many instructors over the years, but we have not had many spiritual fathers. Apostolic ministry has been for us more than helpful covering, more than wise counsel and instruction, more than objective input; it has been all about bringing God's father heart and loving care to our corporate church life.

## A testimony by David Richards

Three times in our history we have invited apostolic teams to come and work on the spot with us to help us see some of the issues that we as local elders were missing either because we were too close to the situation, or just were unable to see what to do next for the further development of the church.

We determined to give them as much room as possible, seeing them as gifts to build up the body of Christ. We released them to be free to examine every area of our corporate life and to look at individuals who needed to be pruned for greater effectiveness, or released further into ministry.

What followed the 1984 review was the release of the church from its doldrums, and an entry into a period of great fruitfulness. As the senior pastor I was greatly helped through excellent communication and clear insight into my own particular strengths and weaknesses. The team's honest, firm but careful pruning helped me see the danger of occasional lapses into unilateral decision-making which had the potential to damage the newly-emerging leadership team. Properly postured, we were now in a better position to make united decisions where all felt they had a contribution to make and would be heard.

We were also helped to see that we had two excellent pastors, proven in the work, who now could be brought out to live off the gospel. This again had the effect of moving the church forward: where we had become stale and somewhat moribund in our house groups, congregational meetings and youth work, the issues and solutions were pointed out.

We can testify that the apostolic visit was the beginning of a big step forward for us: the depth of relationship with the team leader, whom we also received as our spiritual father, made all the difference. You see, we knew that like our heavenly Father, he was *for* us and not against us. It made the whole process so much easier.

There is an issue of control that must be faced here. As elders we have always looked on our role as being one of *stewards* not *owners*. If it had been as owners, we never would have requested the help of outside ministry and would have remained both stuck and impoverished, yet firmly in control. However, in letting go of that control stance, we came into greater release – a consequence of submission to the revealed will of God for us through his servants.

We have lived in the good of that review for a further eleven years, regularly receiving apostolic help with the 'fine tuning' that every church requires. In 1995, we received Bryn Franklin, a prophet from the Oxfordshire Community Churches. His coming to us came about in what can be described only as supernatural circumstances.

Bryn was in a meeting in Oxford in which a number of churches had come together. At the end of the meeting, during a time where people were being prayed for, a man came over to Bryn and said, 'Brother, consider Basingstoke.' This was followed some time later by another man

who prophesied, 'The Lord says, "Go to Basingstoke".'
Finally, a lady approached him and said, 'I see a road
stretching out of Oxford for fifty miles and at the end
there are many doughnuts.' Every lorry [1] driver in the
UK knows that Basingstoke, because of its numerous
roundabouts, is called 'doughnut city'. All three people
were total strangers to Bryn.

Shortly after this, Bryn spent three weeks preaching in
North America. On his return he was about to enter the
front door of the church office in Cornmarket Street,
Oxford, when a man (another total stranger) crossed over
the street, held out a folded piece of paper and said, 'I am
to give you this.' Bryn took the paper and tucked it in his
shirt pocket. At this point he was joined by Richard
Colbrook, with whom he was to go out to lunch.
(Richard, one of the full-time elders, witnessed the whole
proceedings.) As they walked towards the restaurant,
Bryn took out the paper, saying, 'I wonder what this is all
about?' On the paper was written, 'Bryn! Go to Basingstoke.' Within a few weeks Bryn joined us at Basingstoke.

During the next six months we teamed up two other
local prophets with Bryn and they reviewed five of our
ten congregations. In a report to the elders they made
several observations, from which it became very clear to
us all that once more apostolic assistance was required
to help us put in place what the Holy Spirit was revealing
to us.

This time it meant regionalising, re-aligning some of the
elders' roles, and setting in motion clearer lines of
responsibility for leadership teams across the church;
the biggest move being that I now have handed over the
senior leader's role to David Marchment, whom God has
been preparing for over twenty-five years.

This step is allowing me to develop and strengthen the
apostolic team that God has called me to lead, and to give

my undivided attention to the wider and challenging responsibilities that have been occupying much of my time in recent years.

We can honestly say that the whole church has benefited from these reviews; the members have been consulted at every level as part of the fact-finding process. They are included in the reporting-back process through regional leadership teams, house group leaders' gatherings, and the church 'Family Forums'. The directions we have taken have been accepted more readily because of the inclusive spirit and opportunities for both feed-back and prayer.

The result has been blessing: direction and development have been maintained and the church in Basingstoke has continued to fulfill its God-given mandate to be an Antioch church, going to the nations.

## A testimony from Fraser Hardy

The month of the review changed the church here forever: we broke through into clear purpose and definition, while laying a firm foundation that has been built upon ever since. The following statements reflect the thoughts that our leaders have conveyed many times since the review.

The apostolic team was welcomed and given total freedom to look into every area of the church's life, including finances and vision. As local leaders we welcomed this review, but anxiously wondered what skeletons might be uncovered. Although we endeavoured to have everything looking 'right' prior to the review, it soon was evident that our efforts had been futile. The team, under the Holy Spirit's guidance, quickly discerned and uncovered our real state.

So what changed forever? We did. As a church we had been significantly impacted by the charismatic movement during the late 1970s and early 80s. We had seen the gifts of the Spirit (as referred to in Romans 12 and 1 Corinthians 12) rediscovered, distributed, and celebrated with great joy! Our desire to see the restoration of all things led us to start exploring the relevance and place of the Ephesians 4 ministries in our churches today. But we soon found the same hurdles and questions that we had encountered previously concerning the charismatic movement cropping up again. Were they for today, or had their function passed away with the early church? What did these gifts look like and where could we find them? These and many other questions arose, but a growing understanding and revelation of the New Testament helped us see that these gifts were not only vital, but also available to us today. And we were going to need them if ever we were to grow up and come into full maturity in Christ (Ephesians 4:12–16).

This understanding led to a personal journey in which I travelled and stayed with a man who was gifted apostolically. He invited me to travel with him as a 'Timothy' to see what was happening in the churches which he and others were planting and overseeing – churches from the emerging house group/church movement. That year my life changed forever! I saw glimpses of a New Testament church that was born out of relationship and which understood and released leadership. I saw churches and leaders that were connected – not denominationally, but relationally – through the Ephesians 4 ministries received and released to function in their midst.

Scripture came alive to me regarding these gifts to the church, especially that of apostle; and so began a journey of rediscovery that has seen us relate to – and build with – an apostolic leader for the past ten years. Out of this relationship we invited an apostolic team to do a church review in 1988; and what results came forth!

### *Purpose and definition*

There is something safe about building alone (the status quo isn't challenged), but it is a safety that too often has led local leaders into isolation, division and frustration. As local leaders our eyes are often blinded to issues that only Ephesians 4 ministries can see and help us break through.

Within weeks of receiving the apostolic team, we as a church broke through into clarity, peace and order that we had not experienced previously. The team's review revealed issues such as poor communication, leaders in wrong leadership positions, concerns with youth and finances, and our inability to train up leaders. But the team not only revealed areas of weakness, they also gave us new strategy into ways we could change. This enlarged both our vision for blessing the local church and vision for reaching the lost in our city.

Purpose and definition came almost instantly. We realised that just as one received a prophet's reward for receiving a prophet, so too the blessing of receiving and opening our personal insecurities as leaders to apostles resulted in us receiving a special reward from the Lord, we could 'see again'.

This purpose and definition has continued to develop because a review is not just a single event, but rather one aspect of a growing relationship between the apostolic leader and the local church leaders. Apostolic teams now visit us as needed; and I, in turn, travel with them, gaining valuable insight in ways that challenge me to think in broader terms than the local church.

Since that time the church has grown and is currently planting into a new community. Our leaders also help to bring oversight to several other churches. Over the years we have been able to significantly impact both the city and even the nation with strategic conferences – all of this coming about as a direct result of our 'little' doors being opened up to a bigger world.

It has staggered us to discover how narrow and protective we as leaders can become, but a new breeze is blowing in our hearts to let God do what He desires to do with His church. As local leaders we have the final responsibility and say in the local church, but when we walk in relationship with apostolic leaders we no longer find it a place of 'positional' authority – accompanied by fear and suspicion – but rather an environment where we are loved, cared for, and challenged to go further than we ever dreamed was possible.

### Laying a firm foundation

The input of the apostle and his team has both impacted us and left a firm and lasting foundation. Such apostolic oversight has impacted us more than any other ministry, seminar or event because it has been an ongoing relationship – one which is beginning to realise the fulfilment of Ephesians 4:14:

> *'As a result we are no longer to be children, tossed here and there by waves ... but speaking the truth in love we are to grow up in all aspects into him who is the head, even Christ.'*

We are finally growing up!

Just as the gifts of the Holy Spirit have become a natural part of our church life, so too the role of the apostle and the other Ephesians 4 ministries have been established in our midst as part of Christ's gift to his body. As a result, we now are confident to reproduce this in the way we build – in the way we plant and oversee churches – because we have come to see it and experience it as a proven biblical model which will equip churches and leaders most effectively in these challenging days.

### Footnotes

1    Or *truck* for our North American readers.

# *Appendix 1*

## Twenty-One Questions

The following is a list of frequently-asked questions concerning the ministry of apostles. In some cases, the subject matter already will have been covered elsewhere in the book, but it may be useful to present it in this condensed format. The questions are not placed in any order of importance, but the first one seems to crop up the most often.

### 1. *How much authority do apostles have?*

First of all, it is important to establish the true nature of spiritual authority.[1] Other forms of authority (or government) carry with them the power of enforcement, whereas spiritual authority does not. It is dependent on God to back it up – either by means of a demonstration of his grace or his judgement. Paul refers to *'the authority God gave me for building you up,'*[2] which speaks of God's grace at work in those who received his apostolic authority. Conversely, the Scriptures are full of examples of those who rejected God's word and God's messengers and came under judgement as a consequence – a judgement that ultimately meant the removal of God's presence and blessing: the proverbial *Ichabod*[3] scenario.

Apostles, therefore, cannot enforce their authority; they

can only speak it. When Paul commanded the Corinthians to discipline the man who was living in incest, and deliver him over to Satan for the destruction of his flesh, it was up to the church to decide whether or not to obey the command. Had they not done so (and assuming that Paul was speaking God's word to them), it is likely that God would have removed his blessing from that church.

Furthermore, apostolic authority is *relational* authority. In other words, it is limited to those churches who recognise it. Paul said to the Corinthians:

> '*Are you not my work in the Lord? If to others I am not an apostle, at least I am to you; for you are the seal of my apostleship in the Lord.*'[4]

Finally, I believe that the authority of the New Testament apostles was unique in that the canon of Scripture was not complete. In fact, their apostolic rulings – inspired by the Holy Spirit – were actually forming Scripture. Thereafter, it would be the function of apostles throughout the rest of history to draw on those rulings: to exhort and command the churches in which their authority was recognised, but not to go beyond the written Word.

## 2. *Where do you draw the line between the apostle's authority and that of the local elders?*

This is always a ticklish question to handle. At a practical level, the local elders – partly by reason of their physical presence – are the highest form of local church government. Having said that, I have to acknowledge that the apostle Paul exercised all sorts of authority without any appeal to the local elders whatsoever. A classic case of this is when he sent Timothy to Corinth. He didn't ask their permission or their opinion; he simply wrote:

> *'For this reason I have sent Timothy, who is my beloved and faithful child in the Lord, and he will remind you of my ways which are in Christ, just as I teach everywhere in every church.'*[5]

One day, right out of the blue, Timothy turns up carrying a letter from Paul. Clearly, Paul expects the Corinthian elders to receive his emissary.

The key to this question must be found in *relationship*. Paul was the founding father of this church and therefore felt he had a right to act in this way. If this had been an 'adopted' fellowship, his writing in this manner could well have been considered presumptuous and officious.

### 3. What is the difference between the 'Twelve' apostles and the Ephesians 4 apostles?

The 'Twelve' were unique on three counts. First, they were called the *Twelve Apostles of the Lamb*.[6] Jesus personally and specifically chose them, as we find in Mark 3:13–14:

> *'And he went up to the mountain and summoned those whom he himself wanted, and they came to him. And he appointed twelve, that they might be with him, and that he might send them out to preach.'*

Secondly, in Revelation 21:14–20 they are referred to as *foundation stones* in the New Jerusalem. Because they had been with the Lamb, they had become exceedingly precious. Every person who receives Christ as Lord and Saviour also becomes precious (as jasper) and, metaphorically speaking, is included in the wall of the city. But only the 'Twelve' are the foundation.

Thirdly, as Acts chapter 1 tells us, they were eye-witnesses of Jesus' life from his baptism to his crucifixion and resurrection.

The apostles of Ephesians chapter 4, on the other hand, were none of the above. Whereas the 'Twelve' could be called *Resurrection* apostles, the Ephesians 4 type would be better described as *Ascension* apostles, as we see in these verses:

> *'When he ascended on high, he led captives in his train and gave gifts to men. It was he who gave some to be apostles ... '*[7]

They also could be called *Equipping* apostles because their function is to *'equip the saints for the work of service'* (Ephesians 4:12).

### 4. Is Matthias rightly numbered among the 'Twelve'?

Whenever this question is asked, it usually is linked with the issue of whether Paul should have been made the twelfth apostle following Judas' betrayal of Jesus and subsequent suicide. But the evidence for Paul's place amongst the 'Twelve' is very flimsy. The criteria for inclusion in this group is stated in Acts 1:21–22:

> *'It is therefore necessary that of the men that have accompanied us all the time that the Lord Jesus went in and out among us – beginning with the baptism of John, until the day that he was taken up from us – one of these should become a witness with us of his resurrection.'*

There is no evidence whatsoever that Paul was present when Jesus was baptised, nor that he was at Jerusalem when Jesus was crucified and rose from the dead. So Paul fails the test right there. There is, however, a reference to him seeing the resurrected Lord:

> '... *He appeared to Cephas, then to the twelve. After that he appeared to more than five hundred brethren at one time, most of whom remain until now, but some have fallen asleep; then he appeared to James, then to all the apostles; and last of all, as to one untimely born, he appeared to me also.'*      (1 Corinthians 15:5–8)

The context of this passage is a defence of the resurrection, not who should qualify as a member of the 'Twelve'. There were over five hundred who saw Jesus after his death and resurrection: that didn't prove that any of them should have replaced Judas.

While Paul doesn't hesitate to affirm his call as an apostle, he does not at any time claim to have been one of the 'Twelve'. In the absence of even one word refuting the method used to pick Matthias or the resulting choice, we must conclude that he was indeed God's choice in replacing Judas: that he was indeed one of God's chosen *Apostles of the Lamb.*

### 5.  *To what extent are 'signs and wonders' criteria for apostolic ministry?*

There is no doubt that signs and wonders should be a normal part of an apostle's ministry, but that is also true of any ministry found in the New Testament. Philip the evangelist saw *signs and great miracles* accompany his preaching, but that didn't make him an apostle.

The passage that is presented to prove that Paul's apostleship was authenticated by signs, wonders and miracles is found in 2 Corinthians 12:12. Dr Jack Deere, in his book *Surprised by the Power of the Holy Spirit* (Kingsway), has this to say:

'The translation of the NIV does give that impression: *"The things that mark an apostle – signs, wonders and miracles – were done among you with great perseverance."* This translation, however, is inaccurate. A literal translation is, *"The signs of an apostle were performed among you in all endurance with signs, wonders and miracles."*

In this passage Paul uses "sign" (*semeion*) in two different ways. The first use of "sign" in the phrase "signs of an apostle" cannot refer to miracles, for then Paul would be saying that "the miracles of an apostle were done among you with signs and wonders and miracles." What would be the point of such a statement? Paul does not say that "the signs of an apostle are miracles," but rather that "the signs of an apostle" are accompanied by signs, wonders and miracles. If Paul had meant that the signs of his apostleship were signs and wonders and miracles, then he would have used a different construction in the Greek language.'

There are a number of suggestions as to what the signs of a genuine apostle might be. Some think it is supernatural patience.[8] Jack Deere believes it is suffering. Another says it was the great number of people who responded to Paul's preaching of the gospel. I believe it includes all of these, but I keep coming back to two phrases written by Paul in which he is placing a distinction between himself and others, namely: *'I laid a foundation'* (1 Corinthians 3:10), and *'I became your father'* (1 Corinthians 4:15). More than anything else, those two words – *foundation* and *fatherhood* – taken in the context of establishing relationally-based churches, sum up the uniqueness of apostolic ministry.

## 6. Is it justifiable to speak of the apostolic age?

There was a book published about thirty years ago in which the writer, an American, not only rejected the idea of Billy Graham being an evangelist, but also sought to prove that Billy couldn't possibly be sent by God because the gift of *evangelist* ceased with the completion of the Scriptures. This argument is linked closely with a similar claim that the gifts of the Holy Spirit ceased when the New Testament was finished.

Proponents of this view usually quote 1 Corinthians 13:8:

> *'Love never fails; but if there are gifts of prophecy, they will be done away; if there are tongues, they will cease; if there is knowledge, it will be done away.'*

This, they believe, took place around the end of the first century. They also claim (without any biblical justification) that where Paul uses the word *perfect* in verse 10 – *'But when the perfect comes, the partial will be done away'* – that he is referring to the completion of the Scriptures (which they also claim is the end of the apostolic age). Verse 12 is interpreted the same way:

> *'For now we see in a mirror dimly, but then face to face; now I know in part, but then I shall know fully just as I have been fully known.'*

Regardless of the various 'dispensationalist' theories, Ephesians 4:13 tells us that the equipping gifts (apostle, prophet, evangelist, pastor and teacher) are given

> *'until we all come to the unity of the faith and of the knowledge of the Son of God, to a mature* (perfect)

> *man, to the measure of the stature which belongs to the*
> *fullness of Christ.'*

Knowledge has not been 'done away'. The perfect has not yet come. I have yet to meet the man who knows everything. We do not yet have unity of faith. Neither have we come to a *'mature man, to the measure of the stature which belongs to Christ.'* I'm sorry, but we're not there yet!

At the end of the 19th century, a group of Pentecostals residing in and around Bournemouth began to form what became known as the *Apostolic Faith Church of Great Britain*. One of their number, Musgrave Reade, preached a message on the headship of Christ and his ascension gifts to the church – which in particular dealt with apostles and prophets being restored to the church. This was later printed in the church's official magazine, *Showers of Blessing*, and was probably the first publication of this doctrine in twentieth century England. Here is what the Reverend Reade had to say almost a hundred years ago:

> 'Does not the very fact of the apostles and prophets as members in the body – the church – prove that they were designed to continue with the church? Can you conceive of God calling this wonderful body, as the similitude of the natural body? Does God take any members of your body, and say now you have grown up, you do not need them, they cease to be part of your body?
>
> Well then, God has shown you that just as your natural body is the similitude of the mystical body of Christ, then the church was designed to have apostles and prophets, and miracles, and governments, and teachers. They all were to remain in the church until

the church age was finished. I think it is so con-clusive, and that this should not disturb us that God is gradually restoring these wonderful gifts to the restored body, which was sick, and has lain ill for many centuries.'[9]

## 7. *If the apostolic age has not ceased, where is the evidence of apostles in church history?*

Here is a very partial list of apostles after the first century. Between 110 AD and 117 AD we have *Ignatius* referred to as an Apostolic Church Father, and between 100 AD and 140 AD we have *Hermas of Rome* also referred to as an Apostolic Father (*Wycliffe Biographical Dictionary of the Church*, Moody Press). In the fifth century, *Patrick* is called Bishop and Apostle to the Irish (*Great Leaders of the Christian Church*, Moody Press).

We have *Boniface* in the eighth century, called the Apostle to the Germans, and who was martyred in 755 AD by a hostile gang of pagans (Elgin S. Moyer, *The Wycliffe Biographical Dictionary of the Church*, Moody Press). Then there were two brothers in the ninth century, *Cyril* and *Methodius* called Apostles to the Slavs (*The History of Christianity*, Lion Handbook).

Between 1540 AD and 1552 AD there was *Francis Xavier* who was known as the Apostle of the Indies and Japan (*Great Leaders of the Christian Church*, Moody Press). Then, according to Joseph Ritson in *The Romance of Nonconformity* (W.A. Hammond, 1910), we have several leaders amongst the Primitive Methodists of 1815 – also known as the *Ranters* – who were also recognised as apostles. There was *Billy Braithwaite*, the Apostle of North Lincoln who also was known for his prophetic gifts; *Thomas Batty*, the Apostle of Weardale; and *Thomas Russell*, the Apostle of Berkshire. We have *Adoniram Judson* who in 1812 together with his new bride set sail from America for Burma: he was known as Judson, the Apostle of Burma.

At the turn of the century, *Smith Wigglesworth* came to be known as Apostle of Faith. Later on, *Willie Burton*, *Jimmy Salter*, and *Edmund Hodgson*, pioneer missionaries to the Belgian Congo where they planted nearly 1,500 churches, were also referred to as Apostles to the Congo.

## 8. *What does Paul mean in Ephesians 2:20 when he says that the church, God's household, is built on the foundation of the apostles and prophets, with Jesus Christ as the chief cornerstone?*

There are a number of interpretations of this passage which have been proposed.

It has been suggested that the church is built on the whole foundation of the Old Testament and New Testament revelation. In Old Testament times, the prophets are clearly the key figures, called to hear God's word and to speak it to his people. In the New Testament, the apostles occupy the major role of influence, with the prophets taking a less prominent role alongside them.

This interpretation is doubtful, especially in view of the fact that Paul states in Ephesians 3:4 that the mystery of Christ has been revealed by the Spirit to God's holy apostles and prophets – the mystery being that the Gentiles and the Jews now together inherit all God's blessings in Christ. It makes more sense, therefore, to regard these verses as referring to first century AD apostles and prophets.

Another common view (e.g. John Stott, *Essential Fellowship*, IVP) is that the foundation that the church is built on is apostolic teaching. Actually, both apostles and prophets had a teaching role in New Testament times, so this could fit. They certainly were responsible for ensuring that the newly-founded churches held firm to the truth in

Christ. However, this view restricts the apostolic role –
and sees it continuing only through the ongoing teaching
of the church.

I believe a more fitting interpretation is that just as
Christ Jesus is the chief cornerstone in all the complete-
ness of his person and ministry, so the apostles and
prophets are foundational ministries in the church –
planting, teaching, equipping and overseeing the growth
of New Testament churches. The household of God is
built on these foundational ministries – meaning not only
the 'Twelve', but also others (like Paul) who have been
involved in vital apostolic and prophetic roles through the
centuries.

And just as the church continues to depend on the
*ongoing* work of Jesus Christ as the chief cornerstone –
his current work by the Holy Spirit in building the church
– so too does the church need the *other* foundational
ministries of apostle and prophet to continue. We are still
*being built together* into a holy dwelling place for our
God, and the work of the builders is needed as much
today as it was in the early church.

### 9. How should local churches begin to relate to – and subsequently receive – apostolic ministry?

This question probably did not arise very often in the first
century since most churches were established by apostles.
However, it is an issue that many churches must consider
now.

Before any other steps are taken, it needs to be clear
that everyone in the receiving church is fully cognisant of
the biblical truths that support the welcoming of outside
apostolic input and would be open to receiving such
authority. The reason this is so important is that without
such biblical conviction, the whole exercise would rest on

someone's 'good idea' rather than on the principle of faith.

If this conviction is clearly in place, the elders – and especially the senior leader – should communicate, with much warmth and esteem, how they view this apostle and those with him. Jesus said:

> *'He who receives a prophet in the name of a prophet shall receive a prophet's reward; and he who receives a righteous man in the name of a righteous man shall receive a righteous man's reward.'* [10]

The degree to which the local leaders build a 'platform of honour' in the attitudes of the congregation will be the measure of apostolic anointing released to the receiving church. Jesus was unable to perform many miracles in his home town because of their sceptical familiarity (*Isn't this the carpenter's son?*); there was no platform of honour in their hearts, and there was no faith.

### 10. How should one respond to a request to provide apostolic input to a church with a 'history'?

I have received such requests many times – most of which I have had to decline. The first thing I do is 'dig down to the foundations' and find out how the work was started. In other words, I examine the legitimacy of its birth.

On one occasion I was asked to bring counsel to a church where the pastor had fallen morally. A meeting was arranged whereby I could meet with all the elders. Once they were all gathered, I found myself asking the question: 'Now how did this work get started?' The answer was very revealing. Two wealthy, elderly sisters decided they wanted to start a church, so they built a fine building and then advertised for a pastor in certain evangelical magazines. They also advertised for elders by the same method. Within a few months, they had acquired the church Board, who then set about gathering as many spiritual waifs and strays as possible. I also discovered that each elder had left his previous church without receiving the blessing to do so.

Before the evening was concluded, we all agreed that this church was born out of a good idea, but not God's good idea. The work had never received a 'building permit' from the Lord, and therefore rebellion was deeply entrenched in its foundations. The church was duly dissolved and all of its members were received into another local church; none was lost.

Another way of posing this foundational question would be: is this church an *Isaac* or an *Ishmael*? Was it born of the Spirit or of the flesh? In asking these questions, we sometimes discover that it was born out of human need, or to fulfil human ambition. Sometimes it is out of financial need, or the pressure of others. Or it can be born from the heart of God and will be a 'child of promise'.

Other questions I ask myself are: where are the signs of God's 'fingerprints' – his hand supernaturally at work? Is the request for help 'right out of the blue' or has there been a growing relationship with the leaders over a number of months or years? Is the request because the church is struggling and this is their last hope? Are they clutching at straws or have they genuinely set their hearts to pray and believe that this is God's answer?

Has any legitimate authority ever blessed this work? If we start blessing what God has not blessed, we are only going to compound the problem. And probably as important a question as any: has this church been a part of another spiritual family and why is it thus no longer? If the history includes another spiritual family, it is of utmost importance that proper communication takes place between the leaders of both apostolically-led families before any agreement is reached about receiving such a church.

If I believe it is God's will to get involved, it is critical to settle up front the major changes that will need to be made. For instance, it may be obvious that the current senior leader is a square peg in a round hole – trying to do a job for which God hasn't given him the grace. For me to allow myself to be received apostolically without him being made aware of my intentions would be unethical. The same would apply for any member of the eldership. However, that does not necessarily mean acting hastily. Keep in mind Proverbs 19:2: *'He who makes haste with his feet sins.'* The need to build a trusting relationship with the whole church is foundational to any changes that need to be made.

### 11. Given the growth of the church over two millennia, do we now recognise different types of apostles – travelling, semi-local, maintainers, planters, problem-solvers, etc.?

Clearly there is a welcome change in church climate regarding the recognising and receiving of apostles. But I believe we will see a greater release of the apostolic gifting in the church as Christians understand that apostles come in different shapes and sizes; they don't all look like the apostle Paul! We generally have no difficulty in accepting various levels and types of Bible teachers or evangelists, therefore, we should apply the same principle to apostles and receive them for who they are in Christ, whether they be junior apostles, fathering apostles, planters, or any other type.

Every junior apostle, however, should be linked and accountable in some way to a fathering apostle and his apostolic team. The last thing the people of God need is a bunch of 'lone rangers' charging around the country, throwing their weight around, and being answerable to nobody. If Paul, the greatest apostle in history (apart from Jesus), found it necessary to be accountable,[11] I should think that any other apostle – junior or senior – would need to do likewise.

## 12. How would you spot and train potential (up-and-coming) apostles?

That is difficult to answer because there are so many factors involved in the development of apostles. For example, neither Paul nor Barnabas started out as apostles: we read in Acts 13 that they were among the prophets and teachers at Antioch. However, they were already aware of the apostolic call on their lives because we read in verse 2 that the Holy Spirit said, *'Separate unto me Barnabas and Saul for the work to which I have* (Greek – already) *called them.'* I believe the strongest clue that would point towards a person being an apostle-in-the-making is the revelation given to recognised prophetic ministries and their prophetic words spoken over that person's life.

Once this apostolic call is recognised and accepted, that person needs to be drawn alongside a fathering apostle and quality time invested in him – including apprenticing as part of an apostolic ministry team. Every Timothy needs his Paul. And Paul needed Barnabas – who early on searched for Paul in Tarsus and brought him back to Antioch: what a wonderful investment of time and energy that proved to be!

## 13. How fixed or flexible are apostolic teams?

It seems that Paul usually had three or four main players in his team, but that considerable room was made for others. The team was often fairly large in number and included young and old, women as well as men (Philippians 4:2–3), and people from various nations (for example in Acts 20:4 we read:

> '*And he was accompanied by Sopater of Berea, the son of Pyrrhus, and by Aristarchus and Secundas of the Thessalonians; and Gaius of Derbe, and Timothy; and Tychicus and Trophimus of Asia.*'

Even if the team all set out together, it wasn't long before Paul would leave some members behind to do follow-up work, or assign others to go on ahead to prepare for his coming, or send some to deliver his personal letters. There seemed to exist a healthy 'mix-and-match' on Paul's team – which should stand as a good model for us today. I believe that if we want to see a significant increase of apostolic activity, churches will have to get used to receiving those whom the apostles send on their behalf. But for this to be fruitful, great care needs to be taken by apostles to ensure that they send only qualified, trustworthy envoys.

### 14. How do apostolic teams function?

Very simply by assigning the best man or woman for the job! In the case of planting a new church, for example, the best people to get the work off the ground are evangelists and prophets. I'm not saying that pastoral ministry shouldn't be included, but if it came to a choice between a full-time evangelist or a full-time pastor in that initial stage, I would choose the full-time evangelist and let the pastor earn his keep from secular work for a while.

### 15. How do you ensure balance in apostolic team ministry?

The more representative the team is, the more effective

will be its influence. As has already been mentioned, Paul's team included young and old, men and women, and a variety of nationalities and giftings. But an important point to remember is that the balance is in corporiety, not in an individual. In other words, you don't want bland, inept, politically-correct, *balanced* prophets on your team. Bias of gifting and motivation is not a problem to a building apostle. In fact, he welcomes it with open arms: it is expertise that he is looking for. In the same way that a construction superintendent employs people to take charge of certain jobs according to their expertise, so an apostle requires as many experts as possible. A strong team is made up of forceful, mature, proven ministries. In particular, a senior apostle will always make a special place for a godly, gifted prophet, and will want him alongside himself as an indispensable pivotal hub around which all the other gifts revolve.

### 16. *What does an apostle do if a church rejects his counsel?*

This is one of the most challenging experiences an apostle could face. It will force him to ask all manner of questions: was his counsel from God in the first place? Is the church rejecting his counsel as a means of rejecting him? Is his relationship with the church an *Ishmael* (just a good idea) or has it truly been born of God?

If he believes that he and the church in question have truly been joined together in the Lord, he needs to treat the matter with all seriousness and urgency. First, he must never try to defend himself. Second, he needs to view this as part of God's refining work in his own life. As John Paul Jackson said recently:

'God has shown me that I have lost the right to be right; I only have the right to be broken.'

One of his options, however, might be to suggest the church invite a third party who is trusted by both the local leaders and the apostle, to arbitrate and bring counsel. If this turns out to be necessary, both sides need to realise that the trust factor will have been damaged, and that it will take some time before the confidence and camaraderie previously enjoyed will be restored.

In any case, assuming his counsel is right, he should place the whole matter in prayer before the Lord and leave it there, trusting that God will change the hearts of the church leaders. As we observed earlier, spiritual authority cannot be enforced by human means (other than church discipline where excommunication is required). All we can do is speak what we believe is the word of the Lord and then trust him to watch over that word to bring it to pass.

### 17. *To whom are apostles accountable?*

There are at least three clear places of accountability for apostles. The first, of course, is the Lord and his revealed will as contained in the Scriptures. We must never forget that the Bible not only instructs us, it also judges us. And those of us who teach God's word will be judged with greater scrutiny (James 3:1).

Secondly, apostles are accountable to other peer leaders. Even though Paul personally had received powerful revelations concerning the gospel and the kingdom from Jesus (arguably more revelation than anyone else in history), he still considered it necessary to go to Jerusalem and submit those revelations to those who were *'of reputation.'* He wanted to make absolutely certain the gospel he was preaching was indeed the true gospel. Unlike the leaders of various cults and sects over the years, Paul never thought he was beyond being deceived; thus even though he was aware that some of the Jerusalem

212

apostles had become bogged down in a form of Judaeo-Christianity, he still saw the need to be accountable to them. They were not perfect, but he realised that neither was he.

Thirdly, apostles are accountable to the local church that send them out, and to the churches that receive them. This is especially true of modern-day apostles who, because of fast transport, are usually not separated from their families or their church base for long periods of time (as would have been the case for New Testament apostles). Thus the local church is normally in the best position to monitor the apostle's care for his family.

### 18. *Can an apostle also be a prophet?*

I believe the simple answer is yes. As I see it, the role of apostles and elders is one of government. The elder's sphere is local whereas the apostle's sphere is usually translocal. But alongside that government flow the various ministry gifts. For instance, in Acts 13:1 it says:

> *'Now there were at Antioch, in the church that was there, prophets and teachers: Barnabas, and Simeon who was called Niger, and Lucius of Cyrene, and Manaen who had been brought up with Herod the tetrarch, and Saul.'*

So we see that before Barnabas and Saul were sent forth as apostles, they were recognised as either prophets or teachers. Looking at Paul's ministry in totality, it would appear that a measure of *all* the Ephesians 4 gifts rested upon him.

### 19. *Should a local church plant a new church?*

Many do, of course, but my observation is that there often are inherent weaknesses in such plantings – for example, the members of the new church carrying a 'poor cousin' mentality. I think the scriptural pattern is for apostles and their teams to plant new churches.

Special care needs to be taken where a church in a town or small city (with apostolic assistance and direction) slices off a group from the congregation and forms them into a separate congregation. There is a very real danger of independent or 'party spirit' attitudes developing. Everyone involved needs to understand that there are only three constituencies: the cell group, the local congregation, and the corporate (city-wide) family or church. The cell group needs to integrate fully into the congregation, and the congregation needs to see itself as fully engaged with the whole.

### 20. Should a denomination plant churches?

Again, this is commonly done, but to follow the New Testament pattern, it should be apostles who do the planting, and it should always be done relationally, not 'ecclesiastically'. One hazard of planting churches denominationally is that it tends to produce uniformity – in part because decisions often are made by a central board who may function more like religious civil servants than a dynamic apostolic team.

### 21. Is it right for one man alone to be the apostle to a church?

In the New Testament, you almost always find plurality of leadership and ministry. Jesus sent the 'Twelve' and the 'seventy' out in twos. He sent two for ministry and two for practical tasks such as preparing the Passover meal. Peter and John went up to the temple together in Acts 3, and the Holy Spirit sent out Barnabas and Saul from Antioch. Paul's letters repeatedly show him writing from the perspective of a team.

The same principle is true for elders. For example, Paul addressed his *Philippians* letter to the church *including* the elders and deacons: he didn't address it to the pastor. The New Testament pattern is normally apostles to elders, plurality to plurality. This provides great security to the rest of the elders and to the church as a whole.

## Footnotes

[1] Some prefer the term *Christocracy* (the rule of Christ) rather than the term *spiritual authority*.

[2] 2 Corinthians 13:10.

[3] 1 Samuel 4:21 Eli's grandson was named *Ichabod* because *'the glory has departed from Israel.'*

[4] 1 Corinthians 9:1–2.

[5] 1 Corinthians 4:17.

[6] Revelation 21:14.

[7] Ephesians 4:8, 11 *NIV*.

[8] Actually, I think my wife may claim that one.

[9] James E. Worsfold, *The Origins of the Apostolic Church in Great Britain* (New Zealand: Julian Literature Trust, 1991).

[10] Matthew 10:41.

[11] Galatians 2:1–2.

# *Appendix 2*

## Church Questionnaire

1.  **Name** ..................................

    Function in the church .......................
    How long have you been a church member? ......

2.  **Vision for the church**

    (a) Can you define, briefly, the vision for [church name] generally?

    (i) ......................................
    (ii) .....................................
    (iii) ....................................

    (b) Can you define the vision for your particular sphere of responsibility?

    (i) ......................................
    (ii) .....................................
    (iii) ....................................

(c) Can you identify any particular emphasis or thrust in the church's life at present?

. . . . . . . . . . . . . . . . . . . . . . . . . . . . . . . . . . . . . . . . .

(d) What vision do you have for:

   (i) The geographical area immediately surrounding the church building?

   . . . . . . . . . . . . . . . . . . . . . . . . . . . . . . . . . . . . . .

   (ii) The church in the city/town?

   . . . . . . . . . . . . . . . . . . . . . . . . . . . . . . . . . . . . . .

   (iii) The geographical area surrounding your place of residence?

   . . . . . . . . . . . . . . . . . . . . . . . . . . . . . . . . . . . . . .

(e) Do you believe:

   (i) That the elders communicate their heart and vision sufficiently?

   . . . . . . . . . . . . . . . . . . . . . . . . . . . . . . . . . . . . . .

   (ii) That people understand:
   – How to pray the vision into being?

   . . . . . . . . . . . . . . . . . . . . . . . . . . . . . . . . . . . . . .

   – What positive action needs to be taken to

   implement the vision?

   . . . . . . . . . . . . . . . . . . . . . . . . . . . . . . . . . . . . . .

(f) What, in your view, are:

   (i) The three strongest areas of church life?

   . . . . . . . . . . . . . . . . . . . . . . . . . . . . . . . . . . . . . .

   (ii) The three weakest areas of church life?

   . . . . . . . . . . . . . . . . . . . . . . . . . . . . . . . . . . . . . .

## 3. Worship and prayer

(a) Generally, are you happy with the worship life of the church?

. . . . . . . . . . . . . . . . . . . . . . . . . . . . . . . . . . . . . .

Are there ways in which you think this can be improved?

. . . . . . . . . . . . . . . . . . . . . . . . . . . . . . . . . . . . . .

(b) Are you happy with the corporate prayer life of the church?

   (i) What do you understand is the corporate prayer life of the church?

. . . . . . . . . . . . . . . . . . . . . . . . . . . . . . . . . . . . . .

   (ii) How often do you attend a church prayer meeting?

. . . . . . . . . . . . . . . . . . . . . . . . . . . . . . . . . . . . . .

   (iii) Are there ways in which the prayer life of the church can be improved?

. . . . . . . . . . . . . . . . . . . . . . . . . . . . . . . . . . . . . .

## 4. Teaching

(a) How happy are you with the teaching at both congregational and housegroup level, with regard to:

   (i) Content? . . . . . . . . . . . . . . . . . . . . . . . . . . . . .

   (ii) Depth? . . . . . . . . . . . . . . . . . . . . . . . . . . . . . .

   (iii) Variety? . . . . . . . . . . . . . . . . . . . . . . . . . . . . .

   (iv) Delivery? . . . . . . . . . . . . . . . . . . . . . . . . . . . . .

(b) Which preachers/teachers in the church do you most like to hear? Any reason why?

. . . . . . . . . . . . . . . . . . . . . . . . . . . . . . . . . . . . . .

## 5. Pastoral

(a) How would you describe your relationship with your personal pastor?

. . . . . . . . . . . . . . . . . . . . . . . . . . . . . . . . . . . . . .

(b) In the last three months, has he:

    (i)   Seen you? . . . . . . . . . . . . . . . . . . . . . . . . . . . .

    (ii)  Encouraged you? . . . . . . . . . . . . . . . . . . . . .

    (iii) Prayed with you? . . . . . . . . . . . . . . . . . . . . .

    (iv) Corrected you? . . . . . . . . . . . . . . . . . . . . . . .

    (v)  Challenged you? . . . . . . . . . . . . . . . . . . . . . .

(c) Generally, do you think people are:

    (i)   Being well cared for? . . . . . . . . . . . . . . . . . . . .

    (ii)  Being effectively discipled? . . . . . . . . . . . . . .

    (iii) Being provoked in life with God? . . . . . . . . .

## 6. Housegroups

(a) Do you enjoy going to housegroups? . . . . . . . . .

(b) Do you attend housegroups regularly? . . . . . . . .

(c) On a scale of 1–10, how would you rate the following aspects of your housegroup?

    (i)  Care for one another     1 2 3 4 5 6 7 8 9 10

    (ii)  Worship                1 2 3 4 5 6 7 8 9 10

(iii) Prayer                       1 2 3 4 5 6 7 8 9 10

(iv) Teaching/Bible content        1 2 3 4 5 6 7 8 9 10

(v) Participation/Discussion   1 2 3 4 5 6 7 8 9 10

(vi) Social activity               1 2 3 4 5 6 7 8 9 10

(vii) Evangelism                   1 2 3 4 5 6 7 8 9 10

## 7. Leadership

(a) Have you any comments about the style, quality or effectiveness of the lead given by the elders?

. . . . . . . . . . . . . . . . . . . . . . . . . . . . . . . . . . . . .

(b) What aspects of training or equipping have you personally enjoyed in the last two years?

. . . . . . . . . . . . . . . . . . . . . . . . . . . . . . . . . . . . .

(c) Do you have any positive suggestions as to how leadership in the church can be improved?

. . . . . . . . . . . . . . . . . . . . . . . . . . . . . . . . . . . . .

(d) Do you feel supported in your particular leadership role by:

   (i) Other leaders?

   . . . . . . . . . . . . . . . . . . . . . . . . . . . . . . . . . . .

   (ii) The people you lead?

   . . . . . . . . . . . . . . . . . . . . . . . . . . . . . . . . . . .

(e) Are there people presently:

   (i) In leadership who ought not to be there? Why?

   . . . . . . . . . . . . . . . . . . . . . . . . . . . . . . . . . . .

(ii) Not in leadership, but who ought to be?
     Why?

. . . . . . . . . . . . . . . . . . . . . . . . . . . . . . . . . . . . .


## 8. Evangelism

(a) How would you describe the outgoing vision of
    the fellowship?

. . . . . . . . . . . . . . . . . . . . . . . . . . . . . . . . . . . . .

(b) How could the church improve its effectiveness
    evangelistically?

. . . . . . . . . . . . . . . . . . . . . . . . . . . . . . . . . . . . .

(c) Do you have a vision for any particular nation
    personally? Are you encouraged in this?

. . . . . . . . . . . . . . . . . . . . . . . . . . . . . . . . . . . . .

(d) Are you aware of the church's vision for any
    particular nations?

. . . . . . . . . . . . . . . . . . . . . . . . . . . . . . . . . . . . .


## 9. General

(a) Any further comments about:

   (i)  Meetings:

        frequency . . . . . . . . . . . . . . . . . . . . . . . . .

        length . . . . . . . . . . . . . . . . . . . . . . . . . . .

        content . . . . . . . . . . . . . . . . . . . . . . . . . . .

        variety etc. . . . . . . . . . . . . . . . . . . . . . . . .

   (ii)  Relationships

. . . . . . . . . . . . . . . . . . . . . . . . . . . . . . . . . . . .

   (iii) Other churches

. . . . . . . . . . . . . . . . . . . . . . . . . . . . . . . . . . . .

   (iv) Social issues

. . . . . . . . . . . . . . . . . . . . . . . . . . . . . . . . . . . .

(b)  Any observations about the church in general?

. . . . . . . . . . . . . . . . . . . . . . . . . . . . . . . . . . . .

(c)  Any prayers for its future?

. . . . . . . . . . . . . . . . . . . . . . . . . . . . . . . . . . . .

(d)  Any vision you would like to see developed?

. . . . . . . . . . . . . . . . . . . . . . . . . . . . . . . . . . . .

(e)  Any improvements you would like to see?

. . . . . . . . . . . . . . . . . . . . . . . . . . . . . . . . . . . .

(f)  As I see, the greatest need is:

. . . . . . . . . . . . . . . . . . . . . . . . . . . . . . . . . . . .

(g)  The following steps could be taken:

. . . . . . . . . . . . . . . . . . . . . . . . . . . . . . . . . . . .

. . . . . . . . . . . . . . . . . . . . . . . . . . . . . . . . . . . .

If you have enjoyed this book and would like to help us to send a copy of it and many other titles to needy pastors in the **Third World**, please write for further information
or send your gift to:

**Sovereign World Trust**
**PO Box 777, Tonbridge**
**Kent TN11 9XT**
**United Kingdom**

or to the **'Sovereign World'** distributor in your country.

If sending money from outside the United Kingdom, please send an International Money Order or Foreign Bank Draft in STERLING, drawn on a **UK** bank to **Sovereign World Trust**.